Getting a Job

FOR

DUMMIES®

by Joyce Lain Kennedy

WILEY

Wiley Publishing, Inc.

Getting a Job For Dummies®
Published by
Wiley Publishing, Inc.
111 River St.
Hoboken, NJ 07030-5774
www.wiley.com

For general information on our other products and services or to obtain technical support, please contact our Customer Care Department within the U.S. at 800-762-2974, outside the U.S. at 317-572-3993, or fax 317-572-4002.

Wiley also publishes its books in a variety of electronic formats. Some content that appears in print may not be available in electronic books.

ISBN: 0-7645-6787-X

Manufactured in the United States of America

10 9 8 7 6 5 4 3 2 1

1O/QV/QT/QU/IN

WILEY

Publisher's Acknowledgments

We're proud of this book; please send us your comments through our Dummies online registration form located at www.dummies.com/register/.

Some of the people who helped bring this book to market include the following:

Editorial

Senior Development Editor:
Zoë Wykes

Editorial Manager: Rev Mengle

Cartoons: Rich Tennant,
www.the5thwave.com

Production

Project Coordinator: Kristie Rees

Layout and Graphics: Lauren Goddard,
LeAndra Hosier, Lynsey Osborn,
Heather Ryan, Jacque Schneider

Proofreader: Dwight Ramsey

Special Help
Kyle Looper, Molly Goff,
Cynthia Wood, Gabriele McCann,
Kathy Cox, Jackie Smith

Publishing and Editorial for Consumer Dummies

Diane Graves Steele, Vice President and Publisher, Consumer Dummies

Joyce Pepple, Acquisitions Director, Consumer Dummies

Kristin A. Cocks, Product Development Director, Consumer Dummies

Michael Spring, Vice President and Publisher, Travel

Brice Gosnell, Associate Publisher, Travel

Kelly Regan, Editorial Director, Travel

Publishing for Technology Dummies

Andy Cummings, Vice President and Publisher, Dummies
Technology/General User

Composition Services

Gerry Fahey, Vice President of Production Services

Debbie Stailey, Director of Composition Services

Table of Contents

Introduction

● ●

*O*dds are that you have this book because you feel a need to know what works and what doesn't work when putting together a resume and a cover letter for your job search. This need is no doubt true whether you are

- ✔ A new graduate starting out, a person in the big arch of main working years, or a seasoned ace

- ✔ A downsized job searcher, an individual writing a resume and cover letter to support a career change, a transitioning military member, or a displaced information technology professional

- ✔ A novice resume/cover letter writer or a well-experienced professional resume/cover letter writer

In these pages, the classic strategies and smooth moves I've learned in three decades of career reporting show you how to develop and distribute a state-of-the-art StandOut resume and RedHot cover letter that say you're too superior to ignore.

What Are StandOut Resumes and RedHot Cover Letters?

A StandOut resume is

- ✔ Carefully constructed to compete, compel, and capture attention
- ✔ Too skills-rich to overlook
- ✔ Targeted to the job, showing that you can and will do the work
- ✔ Good looking

A RedHot cover letter is

- ✔ Hot-wired to a target job
- ✔ So intriguing that a reader makes room in a busy schedule to meet you
- ✔ An electrifying personal advertising tool that short-circuits the competition

How This Book Is Organized

This book is divided into three distinct parts, plus a Bonus Section. Here's the drill on what each part covers.

Part 1: Getting a Job in Today's Market

This part covers the elements of presenting yourself as a StandOut candidate. You find out how to market yourself, which resume format to choose, and suggestions for essential content material to include (and omit) in your resume.

Part II: Cover Letters That Say You're Hot

Part II tells you why you need a cover letter and helps you break out of writer's block, as well. You also find out how your letter should look and sound, and you get great tips on writing a dazzling opening line for your letter.

Part III: The Part of Tens

For Dummies readers know that The Part of Tens is a collection of single-subject chapters that cut to the chase in a ten-point format.

In Chapter 8, I offer you simple adjustments to quickly improve your resume. In Chapter 9, I give you myths that surround your cover letters and kill your chances of getting hired.

Bonus Section: User Guide

Got a question about using the Resumes and Cover Letters For Dummies software? Turn to this concise guide for answers. From installing the software on your computer to getting familiar with the software's features, the User Guide presents the explanations and steps you need to work with confidence.

Icons Used in This Book

For Dummies signature icons are those little round pictures you see in the margins of the book. I use them to rivet your attention on key bits of information. Here's a list of the icons you find in this book and what they mean.

This icon directs your undivided attention to resume techniques that make you stand out from the crowd.

Differences of opinion are found throughout recruitment and resume writing. Nothing works 100 percent of the time for everyone in every walk of life. This icon reminds you to try to make the best choice for your situation.

These powder-keg tips will make your cover letter burn all the rest.

This icon notes the fundamental facts of cover letter preparation and job hunting. When you need to get down to basics, this is it.

Some of the points in this book are so basic or important that you'll want to commit them to memory. This icon alerts you to those points.

This icon flags information that can make a difference in the outcome of your job search.

Where to Go from Here!

Jump in where the topic looks inviting and applicable — I've done my best to make it all outstanding.

Part I

Getting a Job in Today's Market

The 5th Wave   By Rich Tennant

"I like your resume, Mr. Chan – 4 cups of culinary school, 3/4 tablespoon internship, and a pinch of restaurant management. The only problem I have is finding the pound of dough it'll take to hire you."

In this part . . .

You find out how to choose the best format for your resume and write the most effective content to bring you to the top of any interview scheduler's pile.

Chapter 1

Market Yourself with a StandOut Resume

*Y*ou say that you're ready to step out and find a terrific job? You say that you're tired of selling off a piece of your life in return for forgettable pay in going-nowhere jobs? Or you're fed up with starving as a student? You say that you want a job that speaks fluent money with an interesting accent? Sounds good. But that's not *all* you want, you say?

Such StandOut jobs are going to people who, with StandOut resumes and self-discipline, have found out how to outrun the crowd. This chapter tells why you need a StandOut resume to get a job.

You Want, Well, Everything!

You want a job that puts jingle in your pocket and paper in your bank account. Yes. But you also want *meaningful* work.

I understand. What you want is a job that you love getting up in the morning to do and that pays major money, has first-class benefits, provides self-actualizing challenges, doesn't disappear overnight, and maybe sends you off on pleasant travels periodically. In Hollywoodspeak, what you want is one of those above-the-line jobs that stars you in "Purposeful Endeavor."

Keep in mind that a global knowledge revolution, as far-reaching as the Industrial Revolution, is changing business. And business is changing the job market. No one is immune to getting laid off as lifetime jobs become a memory. The good news is that more resources to help individuals find new work connections have appeared during the past decade than in all of previous history.

What should you do when you want to start a career, or change careers, but you don't know to what exactly? Sorry, but you're not ready to write a StandOut resume. First, you need to clarify your direction through either introspection or professional career counseling. For a jumpstart on mapping out your life's direction, see the sidebar in this chapter: "Help in discovering what you want to do."

Really, Must You Have a Resume?

Periodically, job guide writers, with gunslinging self-assurance, assert that resumes are unnecessary baggage. These critics insist that the best way to find a job is to network and talk your way inside. Put wax in your ears when you encounter these folks — they're shooting blanks. The only people for whom the no-resume advice is okay are those who can leave talk-show hosts struggling to get a word in edgewise. Very few people are extroverted and glib enough to carry the entire weight of their employment marketing presentations without supporting materials.

More importantly, you need a resume because most employers say that you need a resume. Employers don't have time to take oral histories when you call to "ask for a few minutes of time to discuss job opportunities." Those days are gone. A StandOut resume that's easily read and absorbed saves employers time and shows that you're aware of this reality.

Even if — as a corporate executive's child, pal, or hairdresser — you land on a payroll by *fiat* (or decree), somewhere along the way you'll need a resume. At some point, people who make hiring decisions insist on seeing a piece of paper or a computer screen that spells out your qualifications. Resumes are an important first step on the road to the perfect job.

Resumes open doors to job interviews; interviews open doors to jobs.

Tooling Around with Your Resume

A resume used to be a simple, low-key sheet or two of paper outlining your experience and education, with a list of references at the end. That kind of resume is now a museum piece.

By contrast, your StandOut resume is a specially prepared sales presentation. Created as a sales tool to persuade a potential employer that you're the best one to do the job you seek, your resume is a self-advertisement that showcases your skills. With a series of well-written statements that highlight your previous work experience, education, and other background information, your resume helps prove what you say about your achievements, accomplishments, and abilities. It tells an employer you have a positive work attitude and strong interpersonal skills.

As a sales tool, your resume outlines your strengths as a product:

- ✔ The skills you bring to the organization
- ✔ The reasons you're worth the money you hope to earn
- ✔ Your capacity for doing the work better than other candidates
- ✔ Your ability to solve company or industry problems

In every statement, your resume strategically convinces employers that you can do the job, have a positive work attitude, and get along with others. Your resume — whether stored in the rapidly expanding electronic universe or on paper — helps employers to see how they could benefit by interviewing you.

Tailoring Your Resume

When do you need more than one version of your resume? Most of the time. Following the usual approach, you develop a core resume and then amend it to fit specific positions, career fields, or industries.

Nothing beats a perfect or near-perfect match. Suppose a company sports a job opening requiring A, B, and C experience or education. By designing your resume for the target position, you show that you're well endowed with A, B, and C experience or education — a very close match between the company's requirements and your qualifications.

Research is the key to tailoring your resume to the company you want to work for or the job you know you'd excel at.

Help in discovering what you want to do

Does thinking about a career make you feel as if you're stuck in traffic? Then here are a few free Web sites that can help you start moving. These sites offer many tips on career decision-making and management:

✔ **The Career Key** (www.careerkey.org) by Dr. Lawrence K. Jones and other academicians specializing in career development. Much of the work is based on legendary John Holland's six basic personality types. You're given a list of jobs that may be appropriate for each of the personality types.

✔ **Online Personality Tests** (www.2h.com) aren't scored but focus on you as a person who works. (When you get to the site, click on *Personality tests.*)

✔ **Queendom's Best Tests for Career Hunters** (www.queendom.com) doesn't pretend to be scientific, but it does offer a collection of career-focused quizzes, ranging from personality to owning a business. (When you reach the site, click on *Tests & Profiles.*)

✔ **Keirsey.com** (www.keirsey.com) contains links to understanding and taking the Keirsey Character/Temperament Sorter tests, a kissing cousin to the Myers Briggs test.

You can also use the **CACTI** (Core Adult Career Transition Inventory), which is a paper self test by Martin Elliot Jaffe. Order from Public Relations Division, Cuyahoga County Public Library, 2111 Snow Road, Parma, OH 44134. It's inexpensive — call 216-475-2225 for the cost. Adults can use the CACTI instrument at home, as can counselors working with adults in mid-life career transition and discouraged job seekers.

By researching a company and industry to customize your resume and determine new job prospects, not only do you gain the firepower to create a StandOut resume, but you build an arsenal of data points to use in interviews.

Checking out the company

What does your resume reveal about you? Right off the bat, your resume reveals whether you're willing to take the time to discover what a prospective employer wants done that you're well qualified to do. It shows the health of your judgment and the depth of your commitment to work. Your impulse may be to assume that you can write a resume out of your own head and history — that dogged, time-eating research makes a nice add-on but is not essential. Don't kid yourself. At the core of a StandOut resume is research, research, and more research.

For a comprehensive approach, educate yourself about the company's history, growth and acquisition record, products and services, corporate philosophy on outsourcing, sales volume, annual budget, number of employees, division structure and types of people it hires, market share, profitability, location of physical facilities, and how recently and deeply it has downsized personnel. In this usage, *company* means nonprofit organizations and government agencies as well as private companies.

When you know what an employer is willing to employ someone to do, you can tell the employer why you should be the one to do it. *In a tight job race, the candidate who knows most about the employer has the edge.*

Resources for company research — ta-da!

Pulling together the information to write StandOut resumes used to be such a chore that resume writers could spend weeks running down all the facts they needed, visiting libraries for books and newspapers and stock brokerages for annual reports. Mercifully, research is far easier today with a multitude of tools at your beck and mouse-call. To be comprehensive:

- ✔ Line up the usual suspects in printed form — directories, annual reports, newspapers, magazines, and trade journals.

- ✔ Scout the Internet, then use these sites:

  - **American Journalism Review** (www.newslink.org): Useful for researching small companies, this resource allows searching Web news sites, including hometown newspapers across the nation.

  - **Bizjournals.com** (www.bizjournals.com): Another resource to check out small companies, with links to local business.

  - **CEO Express** (ceoexpress.com): This site covers fewer industries than you might expect but the wealth of research and information about each industry is impressive. The site offers a large number of links to business magazines and business news Web sites.

- **CorporateInformation** (corporate information.com): Type in the name of a company, and get a list of sites that report on that company. Or, select an industry, and get a list of companies in that industry, plus news, overviews, and a short write-up about the industry.

- **FreeEDGAR** (www.freeedgar.com): View Securities and Exchange Commission Edgar filings for any company.

- **Hoover's Online** (hoovers.com): A business information database with a ton of information about companies, contact information, key officers, competitors, business locations, and industry news.

- **Plunkett Research** (www.plunkett research.com): An encyclopedic provider of business and industry information, specializing in market analysis and in coverage of market trends, statistics, technology, and leading companies in many fields. View the full database at your library.

- **Superpages** (superpages.com): Comprehensive business information for over 11 million businesses in virtually every city in the United States.

✔ Employee message boards are forums where employees candidly comment on what life is like at their companies. They talk about pay raises, the names of scrappy managers to avoid, impending downsizings, and other items of interest that can help you decide whether you really want to saddle up with certain companies.

Finding out about the job

The ultimate StandOut resume, like a custom-made suit, is tailored to the job you want. After researching the target company and position, you can make your resume fit the job description as closely as your work and education history allow.

Resources for position research — ta-de!

Many companies develop what is called a *candidate specification,* which describes the competencies, skills, experience, knowledge, education, and other characteristics believed to be necessary for the job. Grab this idea and turn it around. Prepare a counterpart — your own *position analysis.*

The content you're looking for to put in your position analysis includes the major responsibilities, technical problems to be solved, and objectives for the position, as well as competencies and skills, education required, and so forth. Find the data for your position analysis in a number of places:

- ✔ **Commercial job descriptions:** Buying job descriptions is pricey but try libraries or friends who work in HR offices. A limited number of free job descriptions are available on the Web; find them with search engines by typing in "job descriptions."

- ✔ **Recruitment advertising** (print and online): Find online recruitment job sites on AIRS Job Boards Directory (airsdirectory.com/directories/job_boards). Look for job ads for the career field and occupation you want. On the print side, newspaper

> help-wanted ads are happy hunting grounds for the data you need to write your position analysis.

> ✔ **Occupational career guides:** The U.S. Department of Labor's *Occupational Outlook Handbook* (www.bls.gov/oco) contains career briefs that describe the nature of the work for popular occupations.

After writing your position analysis, you're ready to roll — in composing a StandOut resume.

When One Resume Will Do — or Must Do

The trouble with creating a custom-tailored resume for every job opening is that many busy and beleaguered people feel as though they can barely manage to get to the dentist for a checkup, buy groceries, pick up the dry cleaning, ship the kids off to school on time, run over to fix Mom's furnace, and generally get through the day — much less write more than one version of an irresistible resume.

It may come down to this: one great resume or no great resume.

You can generally get by with a single version of your resume if you (a) are a new graduate or (b) have a fairly well-defined career path and intend to work exclusively within the lines of your experience.

Even when you allow yourself the luxury of fielding just one resume, you can't put your feet up, watch the sunset, and drink margaritas. With each resume that you distribute, you must attach a personalized cover letter that directly targets the specific job opening (see Part II for more about cover letters).

Chapter 2

Make a StandOut Plan

In This Chapter

▶ Succeeding with a ten-step placement plan

▶ Using personal job agents

▶ Networking inside and outside companies

▶ Following up in professional style

This chapter puts the cart before the horse. The water skier before the boat. The train before the engine.

 Suggestions on how to distribute your resumes before you've written a word come upfront because so much has changed that knowing how you'll *use* your resume could help you do a better job of *writing* your resume.

Market Your Resume in Ten Steps

Follow these steps to get your resume to the right place.

1. **Target your market.** You may not know precisely what you want, but having one to three choices will shorten your search.

   You can be flexible and change directions if opportunity strikes.

2. **Make a master list of job leads.** Identify and research potential employers that may be a good fit. Try to uncover the name of the individual at each company who is responsible for hiring people for the position you want.

3. **Take care of housekeeping chores, such as:**

   • **Get a free e-mail address:** You can get a free e-mail address from Hotmail (hotmail.com) or Yahoo!Mail (yahoomail.com). Be sure to check each and every one of your e-mailboxes every day. Rent a post office box and install a phone with an answering machine if you intend to add that layer of privacy to your search.

   • **College students:** Most college students get a free e-mail address on campus that ends with the extension ".edu" — a dead give-away for student status. Many employers, who really want from one to three years' experience, won't consider resumes with .edu in the e-mail address. Get another address for job hunting, so that you can at least make the first cut.

   • **Consider using split personalities:** Suppose you want to present yourself as a candidate in two occupations or career fields in the same database. For example, you're looking for a job as a convention planner or a market representative. Most databases are programmed to replace resume number one with resume number two, under the assumption that resume number two is an update.

If you want to be considered for two types of jobs, consideration may come automatically as a job computer searches the resume database for keywords. But if you want to double up to be sure, use your full name on resume number one. On resume number two, cut back your first and middle names to initials and change telephone numbers and e-mail addresses.

- **Be mindful of legal issues:** Remember that resume banks must obey civil rights laws: Don't reveal any potentially discriminatory information (age, race, gender, religion, ethnicity) by e-mail to a representative of a resume bank or job site that you would not reveal in a telephone call or during an in-person job interview. Assume the information will be passed on to employers.

- **Use consolidator sites to save time:** Flipdog (www.flipdog.com) and Career Builder (www.careerbuilder.com) are two free services that pull together job listings from many job sites and put them in one place. Additionally, infoGIST CareerInfoFinder

(infogist.com/careerxroads.htm) is a
fee resource that searches hundreds of job
banks, employment sites, and company Web
sites for job leads and company research; a
trial period is free.

- **Bookmark favorite job sites and search
  tools:** Bookmark favorite sites and, on a reg-
  ular basis, make a focused search by job
  title, industry, or geographic location.

4. **Draft your resume(s).** Create more than one
   resume if possible. Shape several different
   resumes: one general version plus several others
   that address the finer points of functions you
   want to do — for example, accountant, internal
   auditor, tax specialist.

   Make sure that your resume contains relevant
   keywords because, in a word-matching keyword
   search, your resume will be stuck to the bottom
   of a database if it lacks the required words.

5. **Draft back-up self-marketing content.** Create
   mix-and-match text blocks for a fast tune-up of
   your resumes and cover letters. Write a variety of
   paragraphs and store them on your computer.
   Need ideas of what to say in the paragraphs?
   Read resumes of others in your field and be
   inspired. Then, when you must quickly put
   together a resume targeted to a specific job —
   and none of your full-blown resume versions are
   perfect — your inventory of text blocks gives you
   a running start.

6. **Draft your cover letters.** Draft several cover letters. See Part II for state-of-the-art tips on writing
   dynamic statements.

7. **Review today's submission technology.**
Telephone an employer about any job that's very
important to you and inquire about that specific
company's technology. When in doubt, paste your
cover letter and resume in the body of an e-mail
message and attach a formatted resume document. That way you're sure that the employer will
be able to read your letter and resume, regardless
of how old the technology is.

8. **Save your resumes and cover letters in useful
formats.** Ready your resume packages for battle
by saving them on your hard drive, and on a disk
if you transmit resumes from more than one
location.

9. **Determine your online resume strategy.** If privacy issues are of concern to you, you may choose
any of several strategies:

   • **Conservatively confidential:** No online post-
   ing of your resume, except as a response to
   specific job listings, or to a targeted mailing
   list of potential employers. You take care to
   protect your identity. You plan to work with
   one or more recruiters (you understand
   that third-party recruiters are paid for finding the best candidates and will likely ignore
   you if you are spread all over the Net and
   can be hired for free).

   • **Moderate exposure:** In addition to the conservative exposure just mentioned, you're
   highly selective about the resume databases and personal job agents to which you
   submit your resume. You may or may not

cloak your identity. You understand the privacy policy of the job sites you select.

- **Full visibility:** You're unemployed and need a job quickly. You post to every logical job site you can find. You want immediate action and are pulling out all the stops.

10. **Keep track of your progress.** Don't let important aspects of your activity get away from you. Keep records of where you send your resume, which personal job search agents are alerting you to the best job posts, and which source of job listings are proving to hold the most potential for you. Make mid-course corrections when needed.

When should your resume arrive? Mondays are busy days, and Fridays are termination days. Try for arrival on Tuesday, Wednesday, or Thursday.

E-mail, postal mail, or fax

A reader asks: "A very simple, but important question: If you are asked to e-mail, fax, or postal mail a resume to a prospective employer, what is the best way to send it?"

When a delivery mode preference isn't specified, I'd start with e-mail because it's easier to inventory in a database and send downstream to hiring managers. Next choice, I'd send postal mail (making sure it is scannable), and, as a last resort, fax.

Branch Out

Networking (read *human interaction that includes employee referrals*) is rated number one in hiring results. That said, put the following tools to use.

Seek endorsement through employee referral programs

If you want fast action and special interest in your candidacy for a job, book your resume for the *employee referral program* (ERP) tour. That is, identify companies where you'd like to work. Start with ten and then move on to a second batch of ten. And so on.

At each target company, network your way to an employee. You may already know some of the people inside a few companies. When you don't know a soul, keep asking someone who knows someone who knows someone. After you identify a contact, enlist that employee's aid in forwarding your name for employment.

At many American companies, large and small, employee referrals are the *number one source for new hires.* Companies pay special attention to ERP candidates because, according to human resource professionals, candidates hired through employee referrals stay longer and assimilate faster than those hired through other methods, including the Internet and headhunters.

What's in it for an employee who refers you? Dollars!
Sometimes, big dollars — starting at $1,000 up to thou-
sands of dollars per referral. And for most of us, that's
not chump change.

Take a dip in a talent pool

Swimming in a company talent pool isn't the same as
trying to capitalize on an employee referral program,
which I describe in the preceding section. Building a network of employees ready to refer you to their companies
could result in a fast job hunt, at least theoretically, while
managing to get yourself in company talent pools could
stretch out your search, or produce future jobs.

What exactly is a company talent pool? Some recruiting
industry consultants describe the talent pool function
as a kind of customer service to woo potential future
employees.

Corporate use of online screening and communication
tools is used to identify well-qualified applicants who
could fill a variety of positions in a given company. Once
tapped for the talent team-in-waiting, recruiters and candidates are supposed to maintain two-way communication (chiefly e-mail and e-newsletters), staying in touch as
needed.

Ask job agents to stand guard

Many millions of Americans change jobs each year, volun-
tarily or involuntarily. Because of diminishing job security,
increased ambition, and new technologies, many people

are locked into a perpetual job search. A job agent lightens the load and notifies you when a job you want comes along.

If you're mobile and have high-demand skills, personal job agents are the best thing since headhunters to add zest to your career management fortunes. In fact, personal job agents prove that the old admonition, "If you snooze, you lose," is no longer universally true.

Just as the devil is usually found in details, the downside is in the ratios: Each personal job agent has a gazillion more registered job seekers than job vacancies. Like 250,000 job hunters and 4,000 job openings. So don't count on personal job agents to come through if you're in a time-sensitive situation (read: *need to get a job fast*).

Follow-Up — An Act of Job Finding

The vast majority of employers — as many as eight out of ten according to some surveys — that use digital recruiting systems (applicant management systems) send out an automatic receipt of your application, commenting that if they want to talk to you, they'll make contact. (To the two of ten who don't — boo!) The response rate of third-party recruiters is unclear, but if you are a potential candidate for a job opening they're trying to fill, you'll hear back fairly quickly; if not, you may get an auto response or none.

Canned response or not, you don't look like a quiz-show winner if you call to ask a transparent question, "Did you receive my resume?" Instead, say some version of:

> *I've had another job offer, which prompts me to ask whether you had planned to contact me within the week.*

Bear in mind, however, that many smaller employers still don't use a digital recruiting system. If you send a resume to a workplace without a digital system (you know because you called first to check), calling later to ask, "Did you get my resume?" *is* a good question.

When you don't "have mail"

If you've had previous contact with the recipient of your resume, the nature of that experience (stranger, referral, friend, telephone call, personal meeting) will suggest whether your follow-up is a thank-you letter or some other kind of communication, such as carrying out the employer's direction: "At your suggestion, I forwarded my resume . . ."

If you've had no earlier contact with your resume's recipient, e-mail or telephone your follow-up. Which is best — e-mail or telephone? I recommend you use the medium that makes you feel most confident and comfortable.

If you've had an auto response and know your resume is in the database, you can ask what happened to it:

> *Was my resume a match for an open position? Was my resume passed on to a hiring manager? Can you tell me which manager?*

After you know that your resume has been routed to a hiring manager, try to contact the hiring manager, who is the one who will quarterback the decision to hire you or not hire you. If your resume was passed on to a departmental hiring manager and you can uncover the manager's name, try calling that manager early in the morning or late in the day. Lunch is not a good time.

Beat Voicemail

What should you do when you try to reach the manager but can't break through voicemail? Leave a short message showing upbeat interest, not desperation:

> *My name is Jane Doe, and I'm calling you because I've successfully outgrown my job, and you have a reputation for running a progressive department. I think you have my resume. If you like what you see, we should talk — 765-432-9999. The best time to reach me today is between 2 and 6 p.m. I look forward to hearing from you.*

Pronounce your name clearly and say your telephone number at a moderate pace. Give the hiring manager a chance to write it down without replaying the message. Otherwise, the manager hears a "garbledrushofwords" and decides "Idon'thavetimeforthis" and moves on.

How often should you call? Some experts suggest calling every ten days until you're threatened with arrest if you call again. But busy employers insist that — unless you're in sales or another field requiring a demonstration of persistence — after you're certain your resume was received, call two weeks later, and then no more than once every six weeks.

An excessive number of telephone calls brands you as a pest. Instead, send notes or e-mail with additional facts about your qualifications, ideas to solve a problem you know the company is facing, or just an expression of your continuing interest in working for the company and the manager.

Everyone agrees that, in this increasingly impersonal world, effectively following-up on the resumes you send out is becoming harder and harder. But the challenge of getting your resumes into the right hands means going beyond transmission to connection with as many recruiters and employers as you reasonably can manage.

Chapter 3

Format Wisely

● ●

In This Chapter

▶ Selecting your best format

▶ Comparing format features

● ●

*R*esume format *refers not to the design or look of your resume but to how you organize and empha-size your information. Different format styles flatter differ-ent histories.* This chapter helps you choose a format that highlights your strengths and hides your shortcomings.

An extensive lineup of resume formats follows. Survey the lot of them before deciding which one best tells your story.

Resume Formats

At root, formats come in three family trees:

- ✔ **Reverse Chronological:** Lists all employment and education, beginning with the most recent and work-ing backward.

- ✔ **Functional:** Shouts what you can do instead of relay-ing what you've done and where you did it.

- ✔ **Hybrid (or *combination*):** Marries both formats.

Take a close look at each of these three formats before
you examine others, of which there are many.

Reverse Chronological

The Reverse Chronological (RC) format is straightforward:
It cites your employment from the most recent back, showing dates as well as employers and educational institutions
(college, vocational-technical schools, and career-oriented
programs and courses). You accent a steady work history
with a clear pattern of upward or lateral mobility.

Strengths: Check to see whether the RC's strengths are
yours:

- ✔ Most popular with employers and recruiters because
  it is so, well, upfront.

- ✔ Links employment dates, underscoring continuity.
  The weight of your experience confirms that you're
  a specialist in a specific career field (social service
  or technology, for example).

- ✔ Positions you for the next upward career step.

- ✔ As the most traditional of formats, fits traditional
  industries (such as banking, education, and
  accounting).

Weaknesses: Take the weaknesses of the RC format into
account:

- ✔ When previous job titles are at variance with the
  target position, this format doesn't support the
  objective. Without careful management, it reveals
  everything, including inconsequential jobs and negative factors.

✔ Can spotlight periods of unemployment or brief job tenure.

✔ Without careful management, reveals your age.

✔ Without careful management, may suggest that you were plateaued in a job too long.

Use: Choose the RC if you fall into any of these categories:

✔ You have a steady school and work record reflecting constant growth or lateral movement.

✔ Your most recent employer is a respected name in the industry, and the name may ease your entry into a new position.

✔ Your most recent job titles are impressive stepping-stones.

✔ You're a savvy writer who knows how to manage potential negative factors, such as inconsequential jobs, too few jobs, too many temporary jobs, too many years at the same job, or too many years of age.

Don't use: Think twice about using the RC if:

✔ You have a lean employment history.

✔ You have work-history or employability problems — gaps, demotions, stagnation in a single position, job hopping (four jobs in three years, for example), re-entering the workforce after a break to raise a family.

The StandOut way to create an RC is as follows:

✔ Focus on areas of specific relevance to your target position or career field.

> ✔ List all pertinent places worked, including for each
> the name of the employer and the city in which you
> worked, the years you were there, title, responsibili-
> ties, and measurable achievements.

Functional

The Functional format is a resume of ability-focused
topics — portable skills or functional areas. It ignores
chronological order. In its purest form, the functional style
omits dates, employers, and job titles. But, employers
don't like it when you leave out the particulars, so contemporary functional resumes list employers, job titles, and
sometimes even dates — but still downplay this information by briefly listing it at the bottom of the resume. The
Functional format is oriented toward what the job seeker
can *do* for the employer instead of narrating history.

Strengths: The strengths of the Functional format are

> ✔ Directs a reader's eyes to what you want him or her
> to notice. It helps a reader visualize what you can do
> instead of when and where you learned to do it.

> ✔ Written after researching the target company, serves
> up the precise functions or skills that the employer
> wants. It's like saying, "You want budget control
> and turnaround skills — I have budget control and
> turnaround skills." The skills sell is a magnet to
> reader eyes!

> ✔ Uses unpaid and nonwork experience to your best
> advantage.

> ✔ Allows you to eliminate or subordinate work history
> that doesn't support your current objective.

Weaknesses: The weaknesses are

- ✔ Because recruiters and employers are more accustomed to RC formats, readers may assume that you're trying to hide inadequate experience, educational deficits, or who knows what.

- ✔ Functional styles may leave unclear which skills grew from which jobs or experiences.

- ✔ A clear career path isn't obvious.

- ✔ This format doesn't maximize recent coups in the job market.

Use: This resume is heaven-sent for career changers, new graduates, ex-military personnel, seasoned aces, and individuals with multitrack job histories, work-history gaps, or special-issue problems.

Don't use: Job seekers with blue-ribbon backgrounds and managers and professionals who are often tapped by executive recruiters should avoid this format.

The StandOut way to create a Functional resume follows:

Choose areas of expertise acquired during the course of your career, including education and unpaid activities. These areas become skill and functional headings, which vary by the target position or career field. Note any achievements below each heading. A few examples of headings are: *Management, Sales, Budget Control, Cost Cutting, Project Implementation,* and *Turnaround Successes.*

List the headings in the order of importance and follow each heading with a series of short statements of your skills. Turn your statements into power hitters with measurable achievements.

Hybrid

The Hybrid, a combination of the Reverse Chronological and Functional formats, satisfies demands for timelines as well as showcases your marketable skills and impressive accomplishments. Many people find the Hybrid — or one of its offspring — to be the most attractive of all formats.

Essentially, in a Hybrid, a functional summary tops a reverse chronological presentation of dates, employers, and capsules of each position's duties.

The hybrid style is similar to the contemporary Functional format — so much so that making a case for distinction is sometimes difficult.

Strengths: A Hybrid format combines the strengths of both the Reverse Chronological and the Functional formats, so check out those earlier sections.

Weaknesses: Its weakness is that it contains more "frills" than a very conservative employer may prefer.

Use: The hybrid is a wise choice for rookies, ex-military personnel, seasoned aces, those with job history gaps or a multitrack job history, and individuals with special-issue problems.

Don't use: Career changers or job seekers needing more appropriate formats, such as Functional or Portfolio, should skip the Hybrid.

The StandOut way to create a Hybrid is to build a Functional format of ability-focused topics and add employment documentation — employers, locations, dates, and duties.

Going beyond the Basic Three

The previous three basic styles have spawned a variety of other formats that I cover in this section.

Table 3-1 gives you a breakdown of which format to think about using based on your circumstances.

Table 3-1   Your Best Resume Formats at a Glance

Your Situation	Suggested Formats
Perfect career pattern	Reverse Chronological, Targeted
Rookie or ex-military	Functional, Hybrid, Accomplishment, Targeted, Linear
Seasoned ace	Functional, Hybrid, Accomplishment, Keyword
Tech-savvy	Keyword
Business	Reverse Chronological, Accomplishment, Targeted
Technical	Keyword, Targeted, Accomplishment, Reverse Chronological
Professional	Professional, Academic Curriculum Vitae, Portfolio
Government	Reverse Chronological, Professional
Arts/Teaching	Professional, Portfolio, Academic Curriculum Vitae
Job history gaps	Functional, Hybrid, Linear, Targeted
Multitrack job history	Functional, Hybrid, Targeted, Keyword

(continued)

Table 3-1 *(continued)*

Your Situation	Suggested Formats
Career change	Functional, Keyword, Targeted
International-job seeker	International Curriculum Vitae
Special issues	Functional, Hybrid, Targeted

Accomplishment format

Definitely not a boring read, an Accomplishment format immediately moves your strongest marketing points to center stage, grabs the reader's interest, and doesn't let go. A variation of the Hybrid resume, the Accomplishment format banners both qualifications *and* accomplishments. This is the format of choice for many executives — particularly in traditionally mobile industries, such as advertising, communications, and publishing.

Strengths: Offers benefits similar to those of functional and hybrid styles noted earlier in this chapter.

Weaknesses: Readers who prefer a reverse chronological style may view the Accomplishment format as too jazzed up.

Use: Go with the Accomplishment format when:

✔ You're considering using a functional or hybrid resume style: You're a career changer, new graduate, ex-military personnel, seasoned ace, or have a multi-track job history, work history gaps, or special-issue problems. The Accomplishment format is especially effective for individuals whose work history may not have been smooth but was, at times, bright with great successes.

✔ You're returning to payroll status after a period of self-employment.

Don't use: If you've climbed career steps without a stumble, use a Reverse Chronological format instead of the Accomplishment format.

List accomplishments in order of importance, making chronology a secondary factor. Close with a summarized reverse chronological work history.

Targeted format

A targeted format, tailored to a given job, is VIP (very important person) treatment. Targeting is persuasive because everyone likes to be given the VIP treatment.

The targeted style is written to match point-for-point a specific job offered by a specific employer.

Strengths: The strength of the Targeted format is that it shows the employer that you're a good match for the position.

Weaknesses: Its weakness is that you may not be readily considered for other jobs.

Use: Pretty much everyone stands out with a targeted resume style. Ex-military personnel can translate military-speak to civilianese, rookies can equate their nonpaid experience to employer requirements, and seasoned aces can reach deep into their backgrounds to show, item for item, how they qualify. This format is a good choice for people with strong work histories but a few ups and downs here and there.

Don't use: The Targeted format isn't a great idea for anyone lazy about doing research — the success of the targeted resume depends on lining up data ducks in advance.

Find out what the position demands and write — fact for fact — how you offer exactly those goods.

If you can meet better than 80 percent of the position's requirements, you have a shot at an interview; if less than 80 percent, don't give up breathing while you wait for your telephone to ring.

Linear format

A Linear format (line by line — hence, *linear*) relates the benefits you offer in short spurts of achievements, winning moves, and the like. An offspring of the Reverse Chronological format, the Linear doesn't get into great detail; it sparks curiosity to meet you and find out more.

This format presents plenty of white space as the hallmark of this achievement-highlighted document. Be advised that career advisers pin a blue ribbon on this format.

Strengths: The *pluses* of linear resumes are

- ✔ Linear resumes are very easy to read quickly, particularly in a stack of resumes a foot high. Instant readability is increasingly important as harried recruiters struggle with the clock, and baby boomers become middle-aged readers whose eyes don't enjoy poring over pages sagging with text.

- ✔ Because the format presents your starring events in a line-by-line visual presentation, your achievements aren't likely to be overlooked as they would be if buried deep in a text paragraph.

Weaknesses: The *minus* is that you can't pack as much information into a Linear format (remember the white space), but, with careful planning and good writing, you can pack plenty of sell.

Use: This format works to showcase career progression — steady as you go. If that's you, use the Linear. Write down your achievements and other necessary data, look at the big lumps of text, and then divide and conquer. Think white space.

Don't use: Job seekers with gaps in employment, too many jobs, few advancements, or scant experience as well as those who've seen enough sunrises to be on the shady side of 50 should avoid the Linear.

Professional format

A Professional format, also called a *Professional Vitae,* is slightly long-winded (say, three to five pages) but factual. It emphasizes professional qualifications and activities. This format is essentially a shortened academic curriculum vitae.

Strengths: The professional resume is mandatory for certain kinds of positions; your choice is whether to send this type or go all the way and send an academic Curriculum Vitae.

Weaknesses: Be aware that professional resumes are reviewed under a microscope; every deficiency stands out. Adding a portfolio that shows your experience-based work skills may compensate for missing chunks of formal requirements. Just make sure that any unsolicited samples you send are high quality and need no explanation.

Use: Professionals in medicine, science, and law should use this format. Also use it when common sense or convention makes it the logical choice.

Don't use: For most nonprofessionals, especially managers, the Professional format is tedious.

Begin with education, professional training, and an objective. Follow with a summary of the main points you want the reader to absorb. Follow that information with details of your professional experience and accomplishments.

Just because you present yourself in a low-key, authoritative manner doesn't mean that you can forget to say how good you are.

Keyword format

Any resume can be a keyword resume. It becomes a keyword resume when you add a profile of *keywords* (nouns identifying your qualifications) anywhere on any type of format. I like front-loading a keyword preface at the top of the resume.

Keep in mind these keyword resume tip-top tips:

- ✔ Use as many valid keywords as possible in your resume, but if you place a keyword summary at the top of your online resume, 20 to 30 keywords are enough in one dose.

- ✔ Computers read keywords in any part of your resume, so if you use a summary, avoid redundancy.

If you use an acronym, such as UCSD, in your summary or opening profile, spell out University of California at San Diego later. If you mention that you have "four years of experience with three PC-based software programs," name the programs elsewhere: Excel, RoboHELP, QuickBooks.

Support your keywords with facts but don't repeat the
exact phrasing in a keyword profile and in other parts of
your resume — vary your language. Repetition must be
handled with thought.

Strengths: Virtually everyone benefits from using a keyword profile — it functions like a skills summary. Job
seekers sending resumes by e-mail or postings on the
Internet should always include keywords.

Weaknesses: A minority of recruiters dislike a keyword
preface. Their objection: "It appears to be a check-box-
oriented approach to doing a resume." This weakness
isn't likely to get you rejected out-of-hand, however. If the
body of the resume supports your keywords (which it
should if it's StandOut quality) and you can do only one
resume, it's worth the risk.

Use: Most job seekers should consider the keyword
option. Technical people can't leave home without it.

Don't use: Top management executives (the $500,000-a-
year-and-up kind) are unlikely to be recruited from resume
databases. Executive recruiters do, however, construct
their own in-house databases. In building these in-house
databases, they may import from public-domain databases
that input information from traditional resumes and other
sources.

Begin with your contact information, followed by a keyword profile, an objective, several strengths, and reverse
chronological employment history.

You may choose not to use a front-loaded keyword profile
but rather a one-paragraph qualifications summary or a
skills section composed of brief (one- or two-line) statements. The more keywords (or skills) in your resume, the
better your chances of being summoned for an interview.

Academic Curriculum Vitae

The Academic Curriculum Vitae (CV) is a comprehensive biographical statement, typically three to ten pages, emphasizing professional qualifications and activities. A CV of six to eight pages, ten at the most, is recommended for a veteran professional; two to four pages is appropriate for a young professional just starting out (see the "Professional format" section earlier in this chapter).

If your CV is more than four pages long, show mercy and save eyesight by attaching an *executive summary* page to the top. An executive summary gives a brief overview of your qualifications and experience.

Strengths: A CV presents all the best of you, which is good, but for people with aging eyes, a CV is reading-intensive.

Weaknesses: Weaknesses in any area of your professional credentials are relatively easy to spot.

Use: Anyone working in a PhD-driven environment, such as higher education, think tanks, science, and elite research and development groups, needs to use this format.

Don't use: Anyone who can avoid using it should do so.

Create a comprehensive summary of your professional employment and accomplishments: education, positions, affiliations, honors, memberships, credentials, dissertation title, fields in which comprehensive examinations were passed, full citations of publications and presentations, awards, discoveries, inventions, patents, seminar leadership, foreign languages, courses taught — whatever is valued in your field.

International Curriculum Vitae format

The International CV is *not* the same document as an
Academic CV. Think of an International CV as a six-to-eight-
page excruciatingly detailed resume. Although it solicits
private information that's outlawed in the United States,
such as your health status, the International CV is favored
in some nations as a kind of global ticket to employment.

The International CV is usually a Reverse Chronological
format that includes your contact information, qualifications summary, professional background, education, and
personal information. Some European countries prefer
the Chronological format, which lists education and work
experience from the farthest back to the present.

Strengths and weaknesses: International employment
experts say that if you don't use this format, foreign
recruiters may think you're hiding something. But keep in
mind that the International CV format intrudes into private areas of your life.

Use: Choose this format if you're seeking an overseas job
and don't object to revealing information that may subject you to discriminatory hiring practices.

Don't use: Individuals who feel strongly about invasions
of privacy or who aren't willing to be rejected out of hand
because of gender, religion, race, age, or marital status
should avoid this format.

Of course, if you want an overseas job and you don't use
this format, you may be out of luck unless you're working
through an American recruiter. The recruiter can interpret your concerns and negotiate for a bare minimum of

personal information. Nationals of countries other than the United States can also use this technique.

Formality prevails with the International CV. In Japan, for example, job hunters still fill out standard forms, available at Japanese book shops. England has a suggested CV form, which is more like the American resume than not.

- ✔ If you're applying in a non-English-speaking country, have your CV translated into the appropriate foreign language. Send both the English and the native-language version.

- ✔ Unless it's untrue, mention in the personal section that you have excellent health.

- ✔ Suggest by appropriate hobbies and personal interests that you'll easily adapt to an overseas environment.

- ✔ Handwrite the cover letter that goes with your CV — Europeans use handwriting analysis as a screening device. If your handwriting is iffy, enclose a word-processed version as well.

In addition, make sure that your cover letter shows a sincere desire to be in the country of choice.

Choose What Works for You

The big closing question to ask yourself after you've decided on a format is:

> *Does this format maximize my qualifications for the job I want?*

If the format you've chosen doesn't promote your top qualifications, take another look at the choices in this chapter and select a format that helps you shine.

Chapter 4

Contents Make the Difference

● ●

In This Chapter

▶ Understanding the parts of your resume

▶ Making each part dazzle the reader

● ●

Deciding what information to put in your resume isn't difficult if you remember the basic purpose: You must show that you can and will provide benefits to an employer. A small lad whom author Robert Fulghum met understood that principle very well. Fulghum wrote about him in *All I Really Need to Know I Learned in Kindergarten*. The boy rapped on Fulghum's door and handed him this note: *My name is Donnie. I will rake your leaves. $1 a yard. I am deaf. You can write to me. I read. I rake good.*

In this chapter, I discuss the building blocks of your resume.

The Parts of Your Resume

To make your contents easy to access, organize the facts into various categories. Here are the essential parts that make up a resume:

- Contact information
- Objective or summary statement
- Education and training
- Experience
- Skills
- Competencies
- Activities
- Organizations
- Honors and awards

These other sections may also be included:

- Licenses, work samples
- Testimonials

To increase the likelihood that your resume will position you for an interview, take the time to understand the purpose of the different resume parts, which I explain in the following sections.

Contact Information

No matter which format you choose, place your name first on your resume, followed by contact information.

- ✔ **Name:** You may want to display your name in slightly larger type than the rest of the contact information and in boldface.

- ✔ **Mailing address:** Give a street name with the unit number, city, state, and zip code. If you're a college student or member of the military who will be returning home, give both addresses, labeled Current Address and Permanent Address.

- ✔ **Valid telephone number:** Use a personal number, including the area code, where you can be reached or where the recruiter can leave a message.

Don't allow children to answer this line. Don't record a clever message — play it straight. If you must share a telephone with kids, emphasize the need for them to answer the phone professionally and to keep their calls short.

- ✔ **Other contact media:** Use any or all of the following, if available to you: e-mail address, mobile phone number, telephone answering service number, and Web page address. However, don't list company resources (such as e-mail or phone number) unless the company is downsizing and providing outplacement support.

Hooks: Objective or Summary?

Your resume needs a hook to grab the reader's attention. The hook follows your name and contact information and is expressed as a *job objective* or as an *asset statement* (also called a skills summary) — or some combination of the two.

The hook tells the recruiter what you want to do and/or what you're qualified to do.

A quick guideline taken from a sampling of six recruiters, as reported in *Job Choices* magazine, is this: "Objective statements are essential for recent graduates, summary statements for seasoned professionals."

What you really need on your resume is *focus,* whether you style it as a job objective or as a summary.

The job objective statement

Weigh these considerations when deciding how to help readers visualize what you could do for them in the future.

Use a job objective when:

- ✔ You're a new graduate or a career changer exiting the military, the clergy, education, or full-time home-making. A job objective says what you're looking for.

- ✔ You have a greatly diversified background that may perplex some employers.

- ✔ You know the job being offered; make that job title your job objective.

The skills summary (asset statements)

A summary statement announces who you are and identifies your strengths. Take a look at the sections that follow for tips on when a summary statement is best.

Use a summary statement when:

- ✔ You're a person with widely applicable skills. Recruiters especially like a skills summary atop a reverse chronological resume because it lets them creatively consider you for jobs that you may not know exist.

- ✔ You're in a career field with pathways to multiple occupations or industries (an administrative assistant, for example).

- ✔ You know that your resume is headed to an electronic database and you want to be considered for multiple jobs.

A summary can be stated in paragraph form or in four to six bulleted quick-hits, such as:

- ✔ Recruited and trained more than 300 people

- ✔ Installed robotics, standardizing product, reducing retraining cost by 16%

- ✔ Slashed initial training costs from $800,000 to $650,000 within one year

- ✔ Created dynamic training culture to support the introduction of a new product

What to Include Next

After you've written your contact information and job objective or summary, build your resume with the following items of information.

- ✔ **Education:** List your highest degree first — type of degree, major, college name, and date awarded.

  If you fall short of the mark on the job's educational requirements, try to compensate by expanding the continuing education section. Give the list a name, such as Professional Development Highlights, and list every impressive course, seminar, workshop, and conference that you've attended.

- ✔ **Experience:** Describe — with quantified achievements — your present and previous positions in reverse chronological order. Include dates of employment, company names and locations, and specific job titles. Show progression and promotions within an organization, especially if you've been with one employer for eons.

- ✔ **Skills:** Skills today are the heart and soul of job finding and, as such, encompass a variety of experiences. These are skills:

  > Collaborating, editing, fundraising, interviewing, managing, navigating (Internet), researching, systematizing, teaching

  And these are skills:

  > Administering social programs, analyzing insurance facts, advising homeless people, . . .

And these are skills:

> Dependable, sense of humor, commitment,
> leadership, . . .

And these are still more skills:

> Brochures, UNIX, "five years," spreadsheet,
> MBA, . . .

Because the term *skills* is widely used in job searching today, a skill is any identifiable ability or fact
that employers value and will pay for. That means
that "five years" is a skill, just as "word processing"
is a skill; employers pay for experience.

Where do skills belong on your resume?
Everywhere. Season every statement with skills.

✔ **Activities:** Activities can be anything from hobbies
and sports to campus extracurricular participation.
The trick is to analyze how each activity is relevant
to the target job; discuss skills, knowledge, or other
competencies developed; and list all achievements.
Make sure that this section doesn't become mean-
ingless filler.

In addition, avoid potentially controversial activities: Stating that you're a moose hunter won't
endear you to animal-loving recruiters. If you've
been able to research the reader and have found
that you two have a common interest, however,
that interest is worth listing on the resume, so
that it can become an icebreaker topic during an
interview.

✔ **Organizations:** Give yourself even more credentials with professional and civic affiliations. Mention all important offices held. Relate these affiliations to your reader in terms of marketable skills, knowledge, and achievements. A high profile in the community is particularly important for sales jobs.

Just as you should be careful about which activities you identify, so too should you be sensitive to booby traps in organization memberships.

- Listing too many organizations may make the reader wonder when you'd have time to do the job.

- Noting that you belong to one minority-group organization may work in your favor, but reporting your membership in five minority-group organizations may raise red flags. The recruiter may worry that you're a trouble-making activist who's willing to exhibit poor work performance and unacceptable behavior in order to create a public issue if you're due to get fired.

- And, of course, you know better than to list your membership in religious or political organizations (unless you're applying for a job that requires such membership). They don't apply to your ability to do the job, and some readers may use them to keep you out of the running.

✔ **Honors and Awards:** List most of the achievements for which you were recognized. If the achievement had zero to do with work or doesn't show you in a professional light, don't take up white space with it; for example, you probably wouldn't list a Chili Cook-Off Winner award (unless applying for a job as a chef).

✔ **Licenses and Samples of Your Work:** If you're in the legal, certified accounting, engineering, or medical profession, you need to add to your resume the appropriate license, certifications, and other identifications required for the position. For a professional resume or CV, you may also need to list descriptions or titles of specific work that you've done or include samples of your work along with your resume. If asked to include samples of your work, be selective about what you send. No-brainer: Make sure that your samples have no obvious flaws or errors.

✔ **References:** *Do not include your references on your resume.* Do create a second document filled with the names, correct telephone numbers, and addresses of references. Supply this sheet only when requested by an interested potential employer.

Because so much information is available about you — probably more than you or I like to think about — make a project of handling your references. Key suggestions include the following:

- **Choose your references carefully.** List references who have direct knowledge of your job performance.

- **Coach your references.** Provide them with your resume. Then, go further: Write a short script of likely questions with a summary of persuasion points under each question.

- **Write your own reference letters.** A letter of reference isn't particularly effective, but it is better than nothing in cases where a company tanks out, your boss dies, or the reference is difficult to reach.

- **Stamp out bad references.** If you were axed or pressed to resign, or you told your boss what you thought and quit, move immediately from spin control to damage control. Try to appeal to a sense of fair play. Sometimes, just saying that you're sorry and you hope that the employer won't keep you from earning a living will be enough. Although, sometimes, it won't.

Top accomplishments

The top 12 accomplishments that most interest employers are

- ✓ Increased revenues
- ✓ Saved money
- ✓ Increased efficiency
- ✓ Cut overhead
- ✓ Increased sales
- ✓ Improved workplace safety
- ✓ Purchasing accomplishments
- ✓ New products/new lines
- ✓ Improved record-keeping process
- ✓ Increased productivity
- ✓ Successful advertising campaign
- ✓ Effective budgeting

No matter how super-powerful you've made your resume, weak or poor references can wipe out your job chances. That's why you write the sample question-and-answer scripts and the reference letters, and that's why you take the first step to patch things up with former adversaries. Your employment is a much higher priority by far to you than it is to reference-givers.

To capture the best job, focus on your best content and present it forcefully. Don't rush the construction of your resume: If you build it right, the interviews will come.

What about salary history and requirements?

Never mention salary on your resume. If a job ad asks for your salary history or salary requirements, revealing dollar figures in a cover letter puts you at a disadvantage if you've been working for low pay — or if you've been paid above market.

Profile forms on job sites and online personal agents almost always ask for your salary information. If you decide to participate, state your expectations in a range ($xxx to $xxx) and include the value of all perks (benefits, bonuses), not just salary, in your salary history.

But first, research the market rate for someone with your skills and experience. Also, find out why the smart money advises against being too quick to pipe up with hard figures on the money you've made and the money you want.

Application forms: Take them seriously

Although many job hunters tend to underestimate the importance of formal application forms, these tiresome profiles are legal documents. Lies can come back to bite you. Stick to the facts as you follow these rules and push some paper:

- If allowed, take the application home; photocopy it in case you spill coffee on your first effort.

- Verify all dates of employment and salaries to the letter.

- Enter the full name and last known address of former employers. If former employers are no longer available, don't substitute coworkers.

- If asked for salary history, give your base salary (or add commission and bonuses), omitting benefits.

- Give a complete employment history in months and years, including trivial three-week jobs that you wisely left off the resume. If you stint on telling the whole story, you leave a loophole of withholding information that later can be used against you if the employer decides that you're excess.

- Unless you have a condition directly affecting your ability to do the job for which you are applying, you need not elaborate on any disability.

- Divulge any criminal record unless your records are sealed; consult a lawyer about the possibility of "expungement" before job hunting.

- Be honest about having collected unemployment benefits (but remember that repeaters are frowned on); if you're caught lying about it later, practice your farewell speech.

- Autograph the application; you've been honest — why worry?

Part II
Cover Letters That Say You're Hot

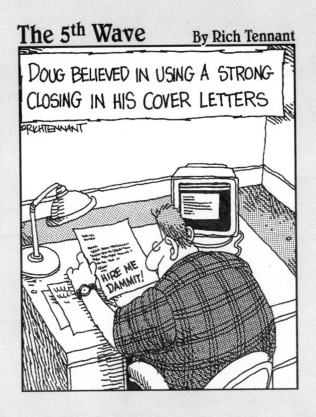

The 5th Wave   By Rich Tennant

RICHTENNANT

DOUG BELIEVED IN USING A STRONG CLOSING IN HIS COVER LETTERS

HIRE ME DAMMIT!

In this part . . .

You know that you're talented. You know that you're capable of doing any job for which you're qualified. What's more, you're pretty sure you're capable of doing a bang-up job if you put your mind to it. But even if you write as well as, or better than, you speak, couldn't you use a little help positioning yourself for the very best jobs?

This part orients you to key cover letter concepts, dissects the makings of a cover letter, and tells you how to create opening lines that are sure to get attention.

Chapter 5

The RedHot Cover Letter Kick-Off

In This Chapter

▶ Why you need RedHot cover letters

▶ Overcoming writer's block

▶ Answers to cover letter questions

A resume should almost never go out alone in the world of employment. A resume needs a cover letter as a companion.

Today's cover letter does far more than ride shotgun for your resume. Today's cover letter is itself a marketing tool, personalized and bursting with vitality. Today, your cover letter offers a great chance to generate an employer's interest in interviewing *you*.

Who Says You Can't Write?

Perhaps you haven't yet gotten the hang of writing contemporary cover letters because you think you can't write your way out of a paper bag, let alone write a letter that will catch an employer's eye. Is that what you think —

don't try because you can't write? I bet you can. And this chapter will prove that I'm right.

All that your protests add up to is the need to expend extra energy into getting your thoughts down on paper — or on a computer screen. Here's some insight into the writing aids and tips you need to do just that.

You Can Write Cover Letters

Here's the thing: RedHot cover letter writing is an attainable skill. It's not Pulitzer Prize writing; it's getting-you-an-interview writing. If your cover letter attracts an employer's interest, the employer will read your resume to confirm a positive first impression. (Conversely, some employers go straight to the resume and, if they like what they see, turn back to examine the other gems of information that grace the cover letter.)

Virtually anyone can learn to write effective cover letters. You can conquer the cover-letter challenge if you really care about improving your career. The difference between RedHot cover letters and run-of-the-mill cover letters is

- ✔ Strong personalization
- ✔ High energy
- ✔ Relevant information
- ✔ Moderately informal
- ✔ A breath of fresh air

A cover letter with each of these qualities is RedHot! What sets RedHot letters apart is a nuance of tone: greater zest, more vitality, more enticement — without extraterrestrial attempts at being clever.

In the competition of today's marketplace, you cannot afford to spend plenty of time perfecting your resume and then throw together a routine cover letter to slap on top. Putting your cover letter on autopilot downgrades your entire self-marketing package. Think about it: your marvelous resume and the boilerplate letter — what an odd couple to send marching out to do battle for you in the job world.

The Advantages of RedHot Cover Letters

Why should you bother to write a RedHot cover letter? Here are 11 good reasons.

- ✔ **Good first impression:** A RedHot letter, as your first knock-on-the-door, grabs the attention of the resume reader: *Hey, you RezReader, slow down, stop, look at me!* The attention flows when you spotlight specific skills important to the reader. A RedHot letter causes the reader to look at your resume with heightened interest by answering the question in most employers' minds — *What can you do for us?*

- ✔ **Focus on employer:** A RedHot letter focuses on the employer, in contrast to the resume that focuses on you. Psychologists are right — we all like to think about ourselves. That goes double for employers. Use words like *offer* and *contribute* over *growth potential* and *career opportunity*. A RedHot letter is a superb employment tool to address the benefits that you bring to the employer.

- ✔ **Matchmaking with benefits:** Salespeople are told: *Customers buy benefits, not features.* Your letter personalizes your qualifications in terms of benefits and conveys them directly to a particular person. You stand out from the crowd by correlating your top skills, knowledge, and achievements with the employer's priorities. You can clearly state why this organization is a perfect place for you to make a contribution.

✔ **Up-to-speed image:** A RedHot cover letter shows that you're in tune with the innovations affecting businesses today. The cover letter is an ideal place to convey that you are on the curve as new business worlds stir.

✔ **Shows savvy:** A RedHot letter demonstrates your ability to understand and fulfill a company's specific needs. It shows that you are smart enough — and committed enough — to scout the company's products, services, markets, and employment needs.

✔ **Presells you:** A RedHot cover letter presells your qualifications, encouraging the reader to imagine you as qualified, personable, and savvy — the type of person to spend 30 minutes of a finite lifetime checking out. A strategic letter prepares the reader to like you. A good cover letter is like having a TV show announcer warm up the audience before the star appears.

✔ **You keep control:** A RedHot cover letter puts control in your hands. It sets up a reason for you to call the employer, if the employer doesn't beat you to the phone. By promising to call, when you do telephone, you can truthfully get past the gatekeeper by saying that your call is expected.

✔ **Adaptability — a practical matter:** Cover letters should be personal, of course. Whenever possible, write to a person, not to a company. Develop several core cover letters — one for each career field. Write a new opening, plug in the target job specifics, and you have a whole new letter.

✔ **Career-changing bonus:** It's not a magic bullet by any means, but your cover letter can be directed to help you change careers. When your most recent work experience is different from the career field you want to enter, use your cover letter to accent your skills that best match the new field. Should you mention why you want to switch? Generally, I wouldn't; doing so just calls attention to your less-than-perfect match for the job. At times, though, it may be necessary.

> *I am well qualified for a small company where wearing many hats is useful. I gained broad experience in different environments during 19XX-20XX at four companies: A, B, C, and D. Each company was acquired, resulting in changes of management. Despite departures of key personnel, excellent references are available.*

✔ **You, a three-dimensional person:** With a RedHot cover letter, instead of being just a name and a set of qualifications, you come alive as a real person with benefits to offer, goals, ideas, and personality. A well-done cover letter suggests that you're knowledgeable, able, talented, and take pride in your work. By contrast, a poor or boring letter suggests that your work will be likewise.

✔ **Reveals critical thinking:** A RedHot cover letter shows the employer how your mind works — how you state your position and then pull everything together in a lucid rationale. In a related evaluation, your cover letter proves that you can communicate in writing — useful for sales letters, memos, and reports.

The Disadvantages of RedHot Cover Letters

There aren't any.

Many Job Hunters Have Writer's Block

Perhaps the reason you're struggling with writing cover letters is that you need to rethink your career goals. You really can't do your best writing about where you want to go until you know where that is. Even when you're certain of your direction, you may still be stuck. This phenomenon is called *writer's block*.

One cure writers use is *freewriting*. When you freewrite, take about 15 minutes to randomly scratch out your thoughts on paper or bang away at your computer keyboard. Don't slow down to organize or edit. After you've pushed your pen for the full 15 minutes, read over your work. Mark ideas, words, and phrases that you can use in your letter. You may wish to freewrite several times until your thinking ink warms up.

Another technique to help you stop staring at a blank page is to answer the following questions. Make notes as you go.

- Whom do you picture reading your letter? What is that person wearing? In what environment is that person reading your letter — a well-ordered office or a room that looks like a teenager's retreat?

- Which qualities do you want to emphasize?

✔ Why will your letter be interesting and important to the reader?

✔ What benefits do you bring to the reader's company?

✔ What special skills or talents set you apart?

✔ Why do you think your employability (person-specific) skills will help you fit into a new company?

✔ How are your previous jobs similar to those you now seek? If the jobs are different, what skills are the same and transferable?

✔ What do you like about the company to which you are applying?

Keep in mind as you embark on the process of writing RedHot cover letters that your first draft is probably going to be shredder-bait, but your editing and refining can fix almost anything.

Presentation

Use a computer word processor and laser printer to turn out a fine-looking letter. Choose standard business size (8½" x 11") paper in white or eggshell. Aim for a letter with no warts, no typos, and clean as a whistle.

Get Ready to Write

If you want your career to take off, make your cover letters terrific! Take more risks, offer more surprises, and find fresh ways to sell your benefits and skills. Pledge to never send out a run-of-the-mill letter again. From now on, you're in RedHot mode!

A time for RedHot cover letters

If you're still in doubt about the power of cover letters, consider this example supplied by Jim Lemke, a staffing and systems consultant who is the technical reviewer for this book. Lemke, a former manager of employment at Walt Disney Imagineering, shares this delightful cover letter story:

At Disney, a job letter arrived from a young man with a simple message:

I want to work for Walt Disney. I am creative. My resume proves it.

The human resources department at Disney sent back a standard software-generated response acknowledging the receipt of the resume and stating that his resume would be scanned into a database. If a suitable job opening arose, he would be contacted.

A second letter arrived from the young man. It said:

I don't think you understand. I really, really, really, really want to work for Walt Disney.

Disney's human resource job computers sent a second message promising to keep his resume.

Soon a third communication from the young man arrived. It was a ransom note, with letters cut from a newspaper. One ear from a mouseketeer hat was pinned to the note:

You still don't get it. I've got the mouse. I want a job.

Yes, the young man got the job. The key is that Disney hired him for his creative mind. Don't try this ploy at Bank of America, but also remember that a cover letter gives you your chance to really shine. A well-written cover letter can help make your ideal job a reality. So, start writing.

Chapter 6

Zooming In on Cover Letter Anatomy

In This Chapter

▶ Connecting the parts of a RedHot cover letter

▶ Writing a letter that says "Hire Me!"

▶ Taking a quiz: Do you know your cover letter's anatomy?

In case you've forgotten or never learned the parts of a job letter, review the building blocks in this chapter.

Contact Information

Your address, telephone number, e-mail address, and URL (Internet World Wide Web address) appear first on the letter. You can place your address in the middle or on either side of the page. Just make sure that your Web address is on a line of its own.

You have a choice about where to place your name. You can either place it (preferably in larger letters) above your address, or you can type it below your signature. The only stipulation: Don't put it in both places. It's a waste.

Computer-friendly cover letters place the telephone number, e-mail address, and Web address on separate lines below your residential address for better scanning. You can also separate two items on the same line.

Date Line and Inside Address

Place the date two lines below your contact information and place the inside address two lines below the date. Aligned with the left side of the page, enter the name of the person to whom you're writing (with Mr. or Ms. designation), followed on the next line by the company name, followed on the next lines by the address. If you know the position the receiver of your letter holds, include that information on the same line as the receiver's name or on the following line.

On the right side of the page, aligned with the inside address information, you can include a line labeled RE: to highlight the reason for correspondence.

Salutation

Your salutation says, "Hello!" in the form of Dear Person-Who-Can-Hire-Me. It's like the eye contact that establishes a connection and begins the dialogue. Do your best to identify the person who will read your letter and address that person directly. Not only does your reader appreciate being addressed by name, but also, this personal bit separates your letter from the ones written by people who didn't take the time to do a little research into the company.

If you can't uncover the name of the hiring manager, write Dear Employer or Good Morning. It's cheerful and feels more personal than Dear Sir or Madam or To Whom It

May Concern. Remember to complete the salutation with a colon (:) to indicate more information to come.

Because no one enjoys reading mail addressed to a generic person (remember all the junk mail you've trashed addressed Dear Resident?), try, try, try to discover the name of your reader. It's courteous, it takes initiative, and it indicates genuine interest in the company and, most importantly, in the job.

Introduction

Your introduction should grab your reader's attention immediately. As the "head" of your letter, it appeals to the head of your reader, sparking interest that will compel your reader to keep reading. It subtly says, "Read Me!" and states the purpose of the letter.

All sorts of rules have been given for ways to start your cover letter. Some say, "Don't start with I." Others advise shock value and creativity, a risky approach for some. The most important rule is to engage the reader's interest. What does the reader need in an employee that you can draw attention to from the get-go? For more information on RedHot opening lines, check out Chapter 7.

Body

The body of your letter provides essential information that the employer should know about you — skills, achievements, and quantified statements about your past accomplishments. These skills may double as the interest-generating element of your letter, as well. The body of your cover letter should be one to six paragraphs in length for eye-friendly appeal.

The body should include a brief background summary of your relevant experience. I suggest including it somewhat like this: "As an accountant at Donne Brothers Company, I accomplished the following: _____" This is information that the reader can get from your resume, so don't spend too much time on it in your letter. But don't be tempted to leave it out. Without this key selling point, your reader may never get to your resume.

The information that you include in the body of your cover letter gives tangible evidence of your potential contribution to an employer. The information provides your reader with facts to digest and arouses hunger for a valuable employee. Make sure that these facts are tasty, enticing your reader to devour your resume and call you in for an interview.

Conclusion

The last leg of your letter aims to stimulate action on your behalf. It gets your reader's blood pumping and legs moving toward the telephone to call you before anyone else does.

Motivating your reader to action requires a sincere "thank you for your time and consideration" and a contact date. Always tell your reader when you will call (no more than one week in the future) to confirm receipt of your letter and resume and to coordinate a time for an interview. Including this information ensures that you'll act; you promised. Your word is on the line. If you call, a potential employer certainly can't ignore you — someone at least will have to move to answer the telephone. And if the news is not good, at least you're not home waiting by the telephone for a call that never comes.

Closing, Signature, and Enclosure Line

The closing section says, "Good-bye." It's the handshake before parting, sincere and warm with promise of meetings to come. "Sincerely" and "Very truly yours" are the most popular, but other choices include "Best regards," "Warm regards," and "Sincerely yours." Don't forget to put a comma after your closing line.

Make sure that you sign off. If your name doesn't appear in your contact information, type your name below your signature (four lines below the closing) so that the recipient has no confusion about the spelling.

If your penmanship runs to chicken-scratch, try to make your signature legible. Any employer prefers to be able to read what someone handwrites rather than trying to interpret it.

Once you've motivated your reader to action, the enclosure line provides a direction. Indicate everything else that you've sent with your cover letter, such as resumes or portfolios. This line directly follows your typed name or signature.

Now Test Yourself

Now, see how much you know. Take the following 40-question true-false quiz, which tests some of the knowledge presented in this chapter as well as your general knowledge of cover letters. Place an X under T (for true) or F (for false).

Your RedHot Cover Letter Anatomy Quiz

True (T)   False (F)

Contact Information

1. Includes your nickname(s)

2. Includes your name (no abbreviations)

3. Includes your direct mailing address(es)

4. Lists all of your e-mail and Web addresses
   on address line

5. Includes your telephone number and other
   numbers (pager, message, office) but
   excludes ex-employer numbers

6. No parentheses placed around telephone
   area codes

Date Line

7. Date is written in full or in brief (abbreviate
   or number months)

8. Date is on its own line two lines below
   contact information

Inside Address

9. Includes recipient's name, spelled correctly,
   two lines under date

10. Includes recipient's job title and desig-
    nations, if any (Ph.D., M.D., C.P.A.)

11. Includes recipient's company (spell out
    acronyms; NASA = National Aeronautics &
    Space Administration)

	True (T)	*False (F)*

Inside Address

12. May hail multiple readers with "Messrs," "Misses," "Mesdames"

13. Includes recipient's address

Salutation

14. Uses "Dear — " "Greetings — " or "Good Morning — " two lines under inside address — greets with friendly tone

15. Includes designation (Mr., Ms., Dr.)

16. Ends with semicolon (;)

Introduction

17. Grabs the reader's attention at once, two lines under salutation

18. Lists who referred you and objective in first line

19. Mentions any mutual acquaintances or previous contact

20. States the position you're applying for by job title

21. Names advertisement (plus publication and date) or contact that led you to apply

22. Lists your top sales points, experience, credentials, or accomplishments

(continued)

Your RedHot Cover Letter Anatomy Quiz

True (T) False (F)

Body

23. Lists personal information verbatim from resume

24. Lists information about you but targets employer's interests

25. Details how your qualifications and qualities contribute to employer

26. Discusses what you didn't like at your last job

27. Discusses how your skills relate to known job requirements

28. Explains why you're applying to this specific employer — what interests you

29. Discusses your familiarity with the industry, including employer's competitors

30. Discusses what you stand to gain (financially) by working with this company

31. You can write as many as six paragraphs or as few as one in the body

32. Discusses salary history and requirements in detail

33. Discusses personal issues and money troubles to evoke the reader's sympathy

Conclusion

34. Thanks the reader for his or her time and interest

	True (T) False (F)

Conclusion

35. Motivates the reader by asking employer to call you at a specific time or date

36. Initiates action by mentioning that you look forward to discussing the position further with the reader

37. Tells the reader what follow-up measures you will take

Closing

38. Two lines below last sentence, uses a complimentary closure statement, such as "Sincerely yours,"

39. When enclosing a resume, "Enclosure: Resume" appears at the bottom-left corner of the cover letter

40. Signature appears at bottom in blue or black ink

Understanding Your Score

Most of the preceding statements are true. However, false statements may have sounded true, so I will comment only on false statements. If you got 35 right out of 40, you're RedHot material.

Here are explanations of the False statements:

1. Nicknames detract from a professional image.

4. E-mail and Web addresses each need their own lines (or to be widely separated by white space

on the same line) because computer scanners can't distinguish them from other number patterns, such as telephone/address numbers.

6. Telephone area codes appear in parentheses, for computer scanners to distinguish them from other numbers in the heading.

12. Messrs., Mesdames, and Miss went out of print with the manual typewriter. Use the name of each addressee (and designation) when possible.

16. Easily confused with the colon, the semicolon (;) divides a two-part sentence. The colon follows salutations to flag more information to follow.

23. Personal information reinforces your chances for an interview only when it is somehow relevant to the position; never repeat your resume in the letter, because your letter's main focus is to snag the reader's interest in reading the resume, not to give away the resume itself.

26. Omit all negative information. Complaining about your last job looks long-winded and unprofessional on paper and may lead to assumptions that you are difficult to work with.

30. Address the employer's financial interests, not yours.

32. Salary issues are complex. Try to save salary talk until the interview, but if you respond to employer's request for salary history or requirements, say as little as possible and speak in ranges: "Am in the $XX to $XX range (Confidential)."

33. People are not hired out of sympathy. Let positive attributes and qualifications speak for you.

35. Asking the reader to contact you is unrealistic.

Chapter 7

Grabbing Attention with Your Opening Line

• •

In This Chapter

▶ Opening statements that stand out from the crowd

▶ Examples of hot properties

▶ Plug-in-the-blank statements to help you get started

▶ Loser opening statements

• •

Suppose you receive a letter that begins

Time flies when you're having fun.

That oldie probably won't entice your reading interest.

But suppose you receive a letter that begins

As Muppet Kermit the Frog says, "Time's fun when you're having flies."

That line is different. That line is funny. That opening lassoes your eyes, roping you into reading further. You keep scanning to find out what message such a whimsical letter could possibly be communicating.

I'm not suggesting you start job letters with frog quotes or other whimsical statements, but I am pointing out that you must work to grab attention. In this chapter, I tell you how to build a fire under your cover letter by opening with words that intrigue, words that excite, words that zing!

Hey, There! Yes, I'm Talking to You

Learn to write openings that fire up the reader and move the reader along without wasting tons of time. Interviewers are overloaded — whole days are a blur for them, and they have no spare minutes to decipher what it is you can do for them.

Consider the harried interviewer poring over an arcane or boring cover letter: "Why am I wading through this slush? I'm not. Let's sail this sucker right into the trash with the other gibberish."

If your cover letter starts off with tired blood, your reader will likely be too bored to keep on reading.

Two Tips for Opening Your Letter

The *best* information to put into your opening line is a name: the name of the letter's recipient or of a mutual friend. Name dropping virtually guarantees that your letter will be read. To get attention, nothing beats the coattails of someone the letter's recipient likes or respects.

Even if the gatekeeping clerical staff doesn't know the names you drop from Adam's house cat, you'll increase your letter's chances of landing on the right desk.

The *second-best* information to put into the opening line is a clear statement of what you want, followed by the benefits you offer — qualifications you have that directly relate to the qualities the hiring company seeks. Skills are mother's milk to opening statements on cover letters.

Don't waste space in your opening lines by citing the source of a job opening notice — "I saw your ad in the *KoKoMo Express* last Sunday." Handle that in the "RE:" line in the upper-right quadrant of your letter.

A Sizzling Sampling

Having trouble launching your first letter? I rounded up some of the best opening lines I could find — from real cover letters — and present them here to inspire you.

- ✔ "During your visit to UCSB last fall, I had the pleasure of hearing you address the issue of FuelCO oil rigs off the coast of Santa Barbara."

- ✔ "We acknowledged and discussed my diverse background when I assisted you through the Internet; I enclose my resume for your consideration."

- ✔ "Since you will soon be working on photo sessions for the Spring catalog, I have enclosed my resume and portfolio to show just how ideal my background in photography and design is for your marketing strategies."

✔ "Juliette Nagy mentioned your company has opened a division of sporting goods and suggested I contact you."

✔ "Your speech was inspiring, Miss Rogers. Soon I will have completed my master's in physical therapy, just in time for your entry-level openings in the PT ward."

✔ "Chaim Isenberg of the Grenwich and Co. accounting firm suggested I contact you regarding opportunities in your warehouse division in Champagne."

What makes these opening lines so great? Some of them mention names. Some connect to a common experience. Some reveal in-depth knowledge of the company involved. All show the letter-writer as a person who cares enough to give time and attention to the presentation made in this self-marketing tool.

Starting Your Motor

Following is a series of plug-in-the-word statements to help you get started.

Name-value phrases

As noted earlier, name-value phrases help you connect your name with the interviewer's through the use of mutual contacts or associations. They give the interviewer one reason to pay attention to your application and a point of reference. If you're naming a person known to the interviewer, be sure to tell that person you're using his or her name.

✔ **You know of no job opening, but the interviewer requests that you send a resume:**

As you requested in our telephone conversation on (date), I enclose a copy of my resume for your review. A quick reading shows my well-developed skills in (a laundry list of your strongest skill sets).

✔ **You call about a job ad, and someone in the company tells you to send a resume:**

As (name of individual) requested during our telephone conversation on (date), I am including my resume for your review.

✔ **A friend or important person suggests you send a resume:**

On (date), I discussed your opening for (job title) with (so-and-so), who suggested I forward my resume to your office. We discussed the position's priorities; they seem to align perfectly with my education and experience. As my enclosed resume shows, my (a skill) and (an experience) will work great in your position.

✔ **You know the job title but can't reach a person by telephone:**

As your office requested, I am enclosing my resume in application for the (job opening title) opening. I understand your company values (a skill), (a type of experience), and (a work trait), and my experience illustrates such qualifications.

If you can't scrounge up a contact or any other "in," try the following general kinds of RedHots to spice up matches between your qualifications and the employer's requirements.

Power phrases

The following opening lines power through with a direct approach and a strong sell that emphasizes belief in yourself and your strengths.

- ✔ "I am particularly well-qualified for your position and would enjoy the opportunity to meet with you to explore how I can enhance your organization."

- ✔ "I was excited to read of your opening for (job opening title) in the (name of publication) on (date). Although we do not share any personal acquaintances, you will see from my enclosed resume that we do share many professional interests and goals, such as (mutual goals). Wanting a more personal introduction, I'm writing to you directly."

- ✔ "For your convenience, I will keep this letter especially brief. The job you're trying to fill has my name on it, thanks to my qualifications in (skills) and (experience)."

- ✔ "Your position for (job title) strongly appeals to me because . . ."

- ✔ "If a meeting confirms my understanding of your open position (job title), I am confident that with my skills in (name skills), I can make an immediate and valuable contribution to (name of employer)."

You want what I am

Similar to direct-mail advertising, this pair of starters sells from the first sentence by directly linking your qualifications with those the firm is in need of.

- ✓ "I understand that your firm is in search of individuals with (skills) and (qualifications); don't you love finding the perfect match? In reviewing my resume, you will find that I possess all the attributes of that perfect match, from (skills) to (experience or attributes). I am delighted to learn of your job opening because I have been searching for a company exactly like yours to make real use of my experience."

- ✓ "Will your (department) reach its (company goal), or will it always (current company problem)? You'll never know without the best person for the job to follow through for you."

Cut to the chase

These opening statements show an awareness of the employer's need for time and efficiency.

- ✓ "My background demonstrates the skills you require in (name of position)."

- ✓ "As my resume shows, I have substantial experience in (field/position/skill)."

✔ "As we discussed earlier, my extensive professional experience can benefit any employer. However, (company name) is of special interest to me because . . . "

✔ "After developing skills in (appropriate to employer, list top skills, accomplishments from cooperative education or student job experience, or make connection between course work and research), as a graduating senior, I have begun to search for a position in (company/industry). I will graduate (date)."

Or

"After developing skills in (appropriate to employer, list top skills, accomplishments from cooperative education or student job experience, or make connection between course work and research), I recently graduated from (name of educational institution) and am searching for a position in (company/industry)."

✔ "I look forward to meeting with you to further discuss my background and to show you some of the (skills) that I have developed."

Network news phrases

You may not know of any job openings, but others in your field do. Don't be afraid to approach fellow members of professional organizations, friends of friends, or other people you know or are known to for help in your job search. Following are examples of some approaches you might use in asking for help.

> ✔ "If any opportunities come to your attention in (field or job title), I would appreciate your informing me. You can expect a call from me on (date)."
>
> ✔ "I appreciate any advice and/or referrals that you could pass on to me."

Leadoff Strikeouts

Every cover letter needs a hard-hitting opener at the top of the page. These real-life cover letter leadoff lines never made it to first base.

Comments that follow in italics are from the employer's view.

> ✔ I was recently let go due to a reduction in force.
>
> *Nothing like starting on an upbeat note.*
>
> ✔ Having recently completed an assignment in the Commonwealth of Independent States (the former Soviet Union), I am interested in pursuing and advancing my career opportunities in this arena.
>
> *Arena? What arena? Here. . . . There. . . . Where?*
>
> ✔ I am currently in search of a job; I have no particular preference in any area, for as you can see from my included resume, my experience includes a broad range.
>
> *One who will take anything masters nothing. As movie pioneer Sam Goldwyn said, "Include me out."*

> ✔ If you or someone you know could use a graphic
> designer, please pass my resume on to interested
> parties, or call me as soon as possible.
>
> *If you're asking me to be your agent, remember, agents
> get 15 percent off the top.*

As noted earlier, you don't get a second chance to make a
first impression. Make sure that the first impression you
make with your cover letter gives the interviewer reason
to invite you in, not write you out.

Part III
The Part of Tens

The 5th Wave   By Rich Tennant

ALTHOUGH EX-PAPERBOY MITCH WROTE A GOOD COVER LETTER, HE HAD TO WORK ON HOW HE PRESENTED IT.

©RICHTENNANT

In this part . . .

*N*o self-respecting *For Dummies* book is complete without The Part of Tens. This part sums up ten tips (more or less, who's counting?) that will help your job search succeed — ways to improve your resume and cover letter myths that defeat your efforts to find work. Read through this information to get you that last mile to the all-important job interview.

Chapter 8

Ten (Almost) Simple Ways to Improve Your Resume

● ●

In This Chapter

▶ Walking in a recruiter's shoes

▶ Discovering that in little words, less is more

▶ Finding success in the 5 percent rule

● ●

So you've finished your resume, and disappointment could etch lines across your brow. No way does your resume show what you're about. When you desperately need the equivalent of a java jolt, your resume seems to have as much punch as a decaf soy latte.

Possibly your resume needs a factory recall, and you should start over. Or, with luck, you may be able to power it up with just a kiss of makeover secrets like those I describe in this chapter.

Use Bulleted Style for Easy Reading

The use of one- or two-liners opens up your resume with white space, making it more appealing to read. Professional advertising copywriters know that big blocks of text suffocate readers. Let your words breathe!

Discover Art of Lost Articles

Although using articles — "a," "an," and "the" — in your resume isn't *wrong*, try deleting them for a crisper and snappier end result. Recruiters and employers expect to read resumes in compact phrases, not fully developed sentences.

The first person "I" is another word that your resume doesn't need. Instead of saying "I worked as the only administrative person on a large construction site," say "Worked as only administrative person on large construction site." Cleaner, yes?

Sell, Don't Tell

Forget the old naming-your-previous-responsibilities routine. Merely listing, "Responsible for XYZ" doesn't assure the recruiter that you met your responsibility or that the result of your efforts was worth the money someone paid you.

By contrast, read over your resume and make sure you have answered that pesky "So what?" question, which is lying in ambush for each bit of information you mention. Try to imagine what's running through a recruiter's mind when you relate that you were responsible for XYZ: *So what? Who cares? What's in it for me?* Anticipate those questions and answer them before a recruiter actually has a chance to ask them.

Frame your resume in results, not responsibilities.

The Five Percenters

Recruiters are wild about snaring the cream of the crop. If you're in the top 5 percent of any significant group (graduation, sales, attendance record, performance ratings) make sure that fact appears prominently on your resume.

Verbs, Nouns, and Writing

Old wisdom: Use lots of action verbs to perk up reading interest in resumes. Later wisdom: Cash in the action verbs for nouns, the keywords that ward off anonymity in sleeping resume databases. New wisdom: Use both verbs and nouns.

Use nouns to construct a keyword profile at the top of your resume. Use action verbs in the body of your resume to liven up your achievements.

Just don't mix noun and verb phrases in the same resume section. For example, here's a list of your resume highlights:

- Founded start-up, achieving positive cash flow and real profits in the first year. [verb]

- President of point-of-sale products. [noun]

- Proven ability for representation of high technology products. [noun]

- Consistently achieved highest profit in 45-year-old company history. [verb]

For *parallel construction,* change the noun statements to be consistent with the verb statements:

- Founded point-of-sale vending company, generating positive cash flow and real profits in the first year.

- Proved ability to represent high technology products.

Strip Out Sad Stories

If your career history looks like the fall of the Roman Empire, don't try to explain a long stretch of disasters on a resume. Save your explanations for an interview.

An exception is when you've suffered multiple layoffs or a company closing within a short period of time. You don't want recruiters to think that you're a job hopper. Add brief notes at the end of comments, such as (Company ceased operation.) (Company downsized 70%.) (Company moved out of state.).

And never apologize on your resume for any weakness that you may observe in your professional self. Shortcomings don't belong on your resume.

Reach Out with Strength

Select the qualifications and past job activities that speak to the kind of job you want and the skills you want to use. Highlight these. If, for instance, you want to transition from military training to civilian training, remain riveted on your training skills without diluting your message by mentioning your ability to use several simple computer programs. If you've muddled your resume's message with minor skills or skills you no longer want to use, get rid of them. Stay on message.

Beware a Wimpy Objective

Imagine an actor striding onto a stage, then standing there like a log addressing the audience: "I came to find out what you can do for me."

Not exactly a curtain-raiser — any more than beginning your resume with simply awful objective statements like: "Seeking a chance for advancement," or "where my skills will be utilized."

Trash the trites: "To obtain a responsible (does someone want an irresponsible?) job with challenging and rewarding (does anyone want dull and unrewarding?) duties."

Draw a line through wussy wording. Your statement can be simple, yet effective: "Management position in finance where more than 10 years' experience will strengthen the bottom line."

Ditch the Cat

If you've included references to your spouse, significant other, domestic partner, or even a family pet on your resume, free your resume from certain shunning by deleting them. These nonworkplace references won't help a recruiter see how you're perfect for the job and, in many cases, they work against you.

Chapter 9

Ten (Or More) Cover Letter Myths That Chill Hiring

* *

In This Chapter
▶ Myths that could make a letter drop dead
▶ Other fictions that sell your letter short

* *

Many people think that cover letters are an optional exercise in the job-finding game. They look at the cover letter as a throwaway piece that no one pays attention to. They take shortcuts and fall for myths guaranteed to show prospective employers that you don't care enough to send your very best. Don't cut corners with your cover letters. Believing the myths that follow can kill your cover letter before it has a chance to sell your skills.

It's Okay to Send Your Resume without a Cover Letter

False! Unless you like to send your resume into other people's trash cans, make sure that a cover letter accompanies your resume. Your cover letter stamps a personality on your resume — a personality that the reader may find tough to reject out of hand.

Your Cover Letter Summarizes Your Resume

False! A summary of the resume and the resume with a summary seem a little repetitive, yes? Use a cover letter to add a warm handshake to your resume and to zero in on why the employer should be interested in you. Your cover letter should put your resume in context — it should draw attention to your strengths and present nonresume material that can make the difference between you and your next closest competitor when the interviewing decision is made.

A Cover Letter Merely Introduces Your Resume

False! Your cover letter is much more than a routing slip for your resume. Your letter is also ultimately a silent force, enticing the reader to scour your resume.

You Can Routinely Use a Generic Greeting — "Dear Employer"

False! Imagine that your job is to screen job applicants, and every letter you read begins with Dear Job Application Reviewer or, in effect, Dear Nobody. Research your target organization until you have the name and gender of the person who will review your resume. Double-check for correct spelling and proper job titles. When you can't uncover the correct name and must rely on a generic greeting, Dear Employer is as good as anything. Don't assume gender by using Gentlemen for your salutation.

Keep Your Cover Letter Really, Really Short — Like a Paragraph

False! The length of your cover letter depends not upon absolute rules of measurement, but upon the amount of content you have to convey. When the letter escorts a resume, I suggest limiting the letter to one page, with one to six paragraphs; when your letter substitutes for a resume, two to three pages is the max.

Devote one paragraph for each salient point. The short-paragraph technique maintains your letter's richness even when skimmed at transwarp speed.

A Handwritten Cover Letter Is Best — It's Personal

False! Handwriting is certainly personal — but for job letters the risks are too high. What are the risks? Employers may assume that you're way behind the times if you don't use a computer's word processor, or they may be unable to read your penmanship. If an employer wants a sample of your handwriting, the employer will request one. Your only handwriting should be your signature at the end, written in black or blue ink. (Colored inks like red or green are seen as unprofessional. Don't risk a job for a color statement.)

Anyone Can Find a Job — If Not, Your Cover Letter Is at Fault

False! Your marketing materials — a cover letter and/or resume — can become an easy focus for your anxieties about a job search. Many of the moving parts of the employment process are frustratingly placed beyond your control: voicemail keeps you from reaching a pre-ferred employer, job openings for your target seem to go underground, interviews fail to spark job offers.

By contrast, the preparation of a cover letter and resume is entirely under your control. When things go wrong, blaming the marketing materials is convenient (although often the blame is well placed). Consequently, job seekers often think that if they can only whip their marketing materials into perfect shape, the other parts of the search will turn out favorably. The truth is, all parts of your search must be up and running.

The Cover Letter Is Your Chance to Talk about Your Personal Life and Feelings

False! Your resume talks about you; your cover letter talks about your intended employer — and how your employer can benefit from the splendid assets you offer. Describe special benefits that set you above other appli-cants. Rambling about personal feelings and situations in an employment letter is a blatant display of self-interest and, worse, is boring. An exception can be made when you're seeking to relocate (provided you offer to pay for the move). Many employers appreciate the desire to be near family as a reason to relocate. No need to go into your uncle's stint in the nursing home — having family in the area is enough.

Include Salary History and Expectations in Your Cover Letter

False! Save the salary discussion for the interview. You can be eliminated at this stage if your salary history is considered too high, too low, or too static. Don't get into it. If an ad requests such information, write that your salary is negotiable and that you'd be happy to discuss the issue during an interview.

Once You Send a Letter, the Employer Carries the Ball

False! No matter how terrific you are, most employers have no time for hunting you down unless they need you right this very second. If you don't get an acknowledgment (probably an automated reply) that your cover note or letter arrived, call or e-mail to confirm.

When Mailing, Use a Standard Business Envelope

False! Before the dawn of electronic magic, folding a letter for a 4" x 9.5" envelope was standard. Now that your documents face a good chance of being scanned and stored by job computers, inserting your letter and resume flat and unfolded into a 10" x 13" envelope is safer. By using a larger envelope, you have a huge edge over thousands of other job seekers who don't know that their marketing materials should arrive scanner-ready.

Paper Quality Always Has a Great Effect on Your Image

True! For a finger-friendly read, paper quality counts. And the more rag content, the better.

Your cover letter and resume paper should match and should be white or off-white smooth paper, 8.5" x 11". Avoid glossy or coarse textures that can cause scanners to misread. Don't use colored paper — especially blue, green, or gray, which may scan in as shades of gray that obscure your letter's text.

Bonus Section

User Guide

- -

In This Section

▶ Installing the software

▶ Understanding the user interface

▶ Writing your resume

▶ Drafting your cover letter

▶ Printing or e-mailing your resume and cover letter

▶ Using the Organizer to remember appointments

▶ Getting help

- -

*Y*ou've just purchased a software program that is both accessible to everyone and easy to use. Welcome to Resumes and Cover Letters For Dummies. Thanks to its ergonomic design and intuitive interface, using the Resumes and Cover Letters For Dummies software is a snap. However, before you jump in with both feet, take the time to read this user guide carefully, in order to avoid mishandling the program and experiencing subsequent fits of frustration.

When you're looking for a job, the more aces you have up your sleeve, the better. Getting your foot in the door of your prospective employer begins with sending out an effective resume and cover letter. With Resumes and Cover Letters For Dummies, you'll be able to write resumes and cover letters in a flash without any special knowledge and tailor them to your exact profile and requirements. In addition, Resumes and Cover Letters For Dummies incorporates various contact list management tools, saving you precious time, especially when it comes to e-mailing your documents.

Resumes and Cover Letters For Dummies allows you to

- ✔ Write customized resumes
- ✔ Draft cover letters adapted to each particular situation
- ✔ Store and manage several documents and their different versions
- ✔ Manage contact lists
- ✔ Print your documents
- ✔ Send your resumes and/or cover letters by e-mail

Installation Instructions

Installing the software from the CD takes just minutes. After you install the Resumes and Cover Letters For Dummies software on your computer, you can run the program from the Start menu or from a desktop shortcut at any time. However, be sure to keep the CD in a handy place in case you need to install the software again sometime.

Minimum configuration

You need the following minimum requirements on your computer to use the Resumes and Cover Letters For Dummies software.

🖊 Pentium 100 MHz or higher

🖊 Microsoft Windows 98, 2000, Me, XP

🖊 16MB RAM

🖊 10MB hard disk space

🖊 Printer

🖊 CD-ROM or DVD-ROM drive

Installing the software

Insert the Resumes and Cover Letters For Dummies
CD-ROM in your CD-ROM drive. Wait a moment for the
program to begin. Then follow the installation steps that
appear on-screen.

If installation does not launch automatically, complete
the following steps for installation:

1. **Click the Start button (located in the lower-left
   corner of your Windows desktop).**

2. **Click Run.**

3. **Type the command** D:Dummies **in the window
   that appears.** If this command doesn't work,
   replace the letter D with the letter associated
   with your CD-ROM drive (E, F, and so on).

4. **Click OK.** The Welcome screen appears.

5. **Click Install to begin installing the software on
   your computer.**

Customer service

Should you encounter any difficulties in loading or using our software, we offer a comprehensive technical support service:

- **E-mail** (`hotline.us@anuman-interactive.com`): E-mail us with your problem, together with as much information as you can supply to aid a speedy response.

- **Web site** (`www.anuman-interactive.com`): Visit our Web site to find information about all our software.

If this introductory user guide does not address all of your questions about the software, please consult the detailed Help files included in the software by clicking the ? button.

Getting Started

In the following sections, we give you an overview of the way the work screen is organized in Resumes and Cover Letters For Dummies. The workspace is divided into these three sections:

- Toolbar
- Side menu
- Display window

Toolbar

The toolbar is located at the top of the work screen and contains eight buttons, each with a specific function. Here, we show you each button with its corresponding function:

Button   **What the Button Does**

 Creates a new letter or resume template from scratch by using the integrated editor.

 Helps you create either a resume or a cover letter and leads you to the job-hunting advice module.

 Enables you to send e-mail with your resume and/or cover letter attached to any recipient in your Contact Management list.

 Opens an organizer where you can schedule dates for sending specific documents and manage your appointments and interviews.

 Displays a window containing information on the software version that you're using.

 Goes straight to the Anuman Web site.

 Provides access to the electronic user guide.

 Exits Resumes and Cover Letters For Dummies.

Menu bar

You'll notice several menus on the left side of the work screen. These menus are

- ✔ **Templates:** This menu, shown in Figure B-1, lets you choose from the different template directories in the Resumes and Cover Letters For Dummies library or the documents that you've previously created or modified (My Resumes and Letters).

- ✔ **Sender Active:** This menu gives you access to the personal data about you and any other users.

- ✔ **Contact Management:** This menu, shown in Figure B-2, enables you to manage any documents to be sent based on who the sender is (if there's more than one user) and recipients.

- ✔ **Template Management:** This menu, shown in Figure B-3, lets you manage the letter or resume template selected.

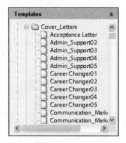

Figure B-1: The Templates menu includes both resumes and letters templates.

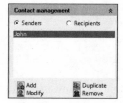

Figure B-2: Select a sender or recipient and sender's data automatically appears in the templates in the form of tags.

Figure B-3: Print the selected template or even search for any template by using keywords.

Display window

The display window takes up the largest part of the screen and allows you to view the selected documents.

The first time you run Resumes and Cover Letters For Dummies, the program prompts you to fill in an entry. Check out the section titled "Managing Contacts" for how to fill out this information.

Creating Your Resume

The Resumes and Cover Letters For Dummies software gives you options for creating your resume. The simplest way to get up and running is to use the Wizard to create your resume and then allow the software to do the heavy lifting for you.

Down the road, however, you may find that you want more creative control over the look and feel of your resume. No problem! Resumes and Cover Letters For Dummies enables you to take complete control over the templates, editing them to your heart's desire.

Using the Wizard

One of the options available to you when you start the program is the Wizard that guides you through the process of creating your resume. To start the Wizard, just click the Create Your Resume button in the Welcome screen, as shown in Figure B-4.

What do you want to do?

Create Your Resume

Create Your Letter

Good Advice For Job-Hunting

Close

Do not display this window on startup

Figure B-4: The Wizard provides easy access to the program's functions.

You can also start the Wizard at any time by clicking the Wizard button on the toolbar.

The Wizard allows you to automatically create your resume according to a template that you select. To create a custom resume with the help of the Wizard, just follow these steps.

1. **Choose the type of resume that you want by checking the relevant box.**

   Here are the different formats of resumes included in the Wizard, as shown in Figure B-5:

   - **Reverse Chronological:** This format cites your employment history, beginning with the most recent and working backward. This format shows dates, employers, and education, as well as a steady work history with upward or lateral mobility.

   - **Functional:** This format creates a resume of ability-focused topics and ignores chronological order. The functional style often omits dates, employers, and job titles or downplays this information by briefly listing it at the bottom of the resume. This format is oriented toward what the job seeker can *do* for the employer, not the candidate's history.

   - **Hybrid:** This format is a combination of Reverse Chronological and Functional formats that satisfies timelines, marketable skills, and accomplishments. In a Hybrid, a functional summary tops a reverse chronological giving dates, employers, and duties.

Figure B-5: There are 5 basic types of resumes in the Wizard.

- **Accomplishment:** This format definitely highlights your strong points. If you want a rhyme to remember: Use flash and dash to go for cash. The Accomplishment format features both qualifications *and* accomplishments. This is the format of choice for many executives.

- **Targeted:** This format targets a given job and is persuasive because it gives the reader VIP treatment. The targeted style is written to match point-for-point a specific job offered by a specific employer.

2. **After choosing one of the five options, click the Next button.**

   The Sender window appears. To return to the previous window at any time and change your choices, click the Back button.

3. **Enter your personal contact information in the Sender window just as you want it to appear on your resume and then click the Next button.**

The Sender window appears when the software starts, and that's a great time to fill in your information. If you already filled in your personal information, simply ensure that the information is correct before clicking Next.

4. **In the Profile window, click the + sign to the left of Position in the Profile window's tree structure and then select Default.**

   Text boxes appear for Job Title and Objective on the right side of the screen, as shown in Figure B-6.

5. **Fill in the name of the job you're applying for in the Job Title box.**

   The job title will be prominently displayed as the eye catcher for your resume. An example of a job title is Assistant Retail Manager.

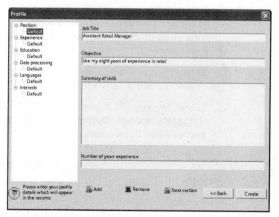

Figure B-6: The Profile window allows you to fill in information specific to the job for which you're applying.

6. **In the Objective box, enter the objectives of your job search.**

   An example objective is "Position as assistant retail manager using my eight years of experience in retail, technical sales, and software."

7. **Click the + sign to the left of Experience in the Profile window's tree structure and then select Default.**

   Text boxes appear for time period, company, function, mission, achievements, competencies, and assets.

8. **Fill in information that describes your work experience in the applicable text boxes.**

   If you're working in the Reverse Chronological resume template, enter all dates, such as July 2001 to October 2003.

9. **If you have more work experience for your resume, click the Add button and then click the new Default entry that appears under Experience.**

10. **Repeat Steps 7 and 8 until you input all your experience.**

11. **Select the remaining sections of the resume in the tree structure in the same way and add the rest of your information.**

You can navigate from one section to the next by clicking Next section.

You can also edit information on the Profile page, as
follows:

- ✔ **Delete part of a section, such as a particular professional experience:** Click on the section in the
  tree structure on the left to select it and then click
  the Remove button.

- ✔ **Change information in a particular section:** Click it
  and change the information directly in the fields displayed on the right and then move on to any other
  sections you want to change.

After you fill in all the sections in the Profile window, click
Create to automatically create your resume. You're then
taken to the software's main screen, where you can see
your resume on the right, completely filled in with the
chosen layout!

If you want to change your resume by adding any missing
information, click the template in the main screen to
open your resume in the word processor.

If you want to change your resume's layout, click the
Wizard button in the browser bar, reopen Create Your
Resume, and change the template selected. All the
information is saved, so simply click Next in the succes-
sive windows and then click Create to display your new
resume.

To add your resume directly to your mailing list, click
Add to Mailing List in the Contact management window.

Here are some useful things to know about the Resumes and Cover Letters For Dummies software:

- ✔ As soon as you enter details in the fields of the Profile screen, the information is automatically saved, even if you accidentally click on another section or button.

- ✔ A confirmation message appears if you click Remove to delete specific information.

- ✔ If a section isn't part of a specific template, that section isn't displayed, even if you've already entered the information. For example, although both the Job Title and Objective fields appear in the first section (Position), the two are rarely shown together in the same resume.

- ✔ Not every resume template uses the same sections; but all sections of the Profile window are ultimately used in one template or another, which is why filling them all in is a good idea.

Customizing a template

One of the major advantages of Resumes and Cover Letters For Dummies is that you can choose from dozens of templates divided into countless professional categories.

Each template is unique in its layout and content. Browse through the templates, and you're bound to come across the ideal presentation and layout to meet your needs.

After you choose a suitable template, you can change it to your heart's content.

Creating your Profile

You need to enter various elements to customize your profile. If you haven't created a profile with the Wizard, you can do so by following the next set of steps. The information you enter in the Profile window appears automatically in the resumes and cover letters templates, which simplifies the process.

1. **Click the double arrow on the Sender Active menu to expand it, if necessary, and then click the Profile link.**

   In the Profile window that appears, you can enter all the elements making up the active sender's profile: position, experience, education, data processing, languages, interests.

2. **Click the + of the tree structure of the Profile window of the resume section you want to define or change to expand it, if necessary.**

3. **Select the Default element that you want to change or define by clicking it.**

4. **Enter your information in all the fields.**

5. **Click the Add button to put more details in each section of your profile.**

   For more details about creating a profile, check out the previous section, "Using the Wizard."

If you want to delete a section from your profile, click to select it and then click the Remove button.

After you define the first sender, any time you click on a different sender in the Contact Management menu, he or she will be defined as Sender Active and the corresponding profile will automatically replace the predefined templates.

Saving your profile as the active sender

Before you can save your profile as the active sender, you have to fill in the personal entry form that opens when you first run the software. If you haven't filled in the information yet or if you want to change the information, proceed as follows.

1. **Click the double arrow of the Contact Management menu if the menu isn't already visible.**

2. **Select the Senders option and then click Add to display the personal information window.**

3. **Fill in the different fields for your contact details.**

4. **Click OK after you finish.**

   Tags show up in your resume or cover letter representing your information, as shown in Figure B-7.

Figure B-7: The information you enter in the fields appears in your resumes and cover letters in the form of tags.

You can change this entry at any time or create another form for either yourself or someone else.

After you finish your entry, some of your contact details appear in the Sender Active list.

Using the integrated text editor for a resume

You can customize your resume even more. To do so, Resumes and Cover Letters For Dummies comes complete with a particularly effective, easy-to-use text editor.

1. **Select a resume template in the Templates menu.**

2. **Click the resume's contents to display them in a new window (the text editor).**

   The text editor, as shown in Figure B-8, works in a way similar to traditional word processors, such as Microsoft Word.

3. **Make all the changes you want by using the editor.**

4. **After you finish with your changes, close the window.**

   The software asks whether you want to save the changes to the letter or resume. If so, click Yes.

5. **The software automatically takes you back to the previously chosen letter or resume template.**

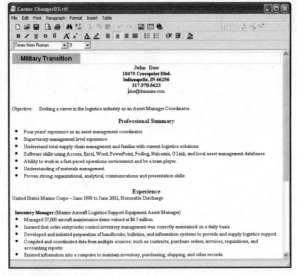

Figure B-8: The text editor enables you to personalize the layout of your resume.

You may have noticed that the template hasn't changed and doesn't show the changes you made with the text editor. When you modify a template, the template is automatically saved in the My Resumes and Letters section of the Templates folder. (You can find this at the bottom of the Templates menu tree structure.)

To display the template you just changed in My Resumes and Letters, you need to refresh the templates. Here's how.

1. **Click the Refresh button in the Template Management menu.**

2. **Return to Templates/My Resumes and Letters to find your modified resume.**

3. To delete a resume template, select the template
   in My Resumes and Letters and then click the
   Remove button in the Template Management
   menu.

Drafting a Cover Letter

A good cover letter can be the difference between getting
an interview and having your resume filed in the round
file. The Resumes and Cover Letters For Dummies software gives you the option of using the Wizard or modify-
ing an existing template to suit your needs.

Using the Wizard

The Resumes and Cover Letters For Dummies Wizard
enables you to automatically create, save, customize, and
address a cover letter according to the information you
enter.

To start working on your cover letter, just click the Create
Your Letter button. Then follow these steps:

1. In the Sender window that appears, enter your
   personal contact information as you want it to
   appear on your letter. When you're satisfied,
   click the Next button to continue.

   Or, if you already entered your information at a
   previous time, you can simply check the information and click the Next button.

   The Recipient window appears, as shown in
   Figure B-9, where you enter the contact details of
   the person intended to receive your cover letter.

   Anytime you want to change information in the
   previous window, click the Back button.

Figure B-9: The information you enter in the Recipient window will appear in the Contact Management menu under Recipients.

2. **Fill in all the required information in the Recipient window and then click the Next button.**

   The Create Your Letter window appears, as shown in Figure B-10.

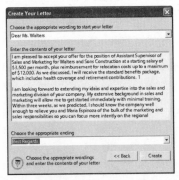

Figure B-10: In the Create Your Letter window, just add your own text, which you can change in the text editor afterwards.

3. **Select a salutation from the Choose the Appropriate Wording to Start Your Letter drop-down list at the top of the window.**

   The name of the letter's recipient is automatically added to the letter according to the details entered in the Recipient window. For example, if you choose "Dear Ms." from the drop-down list and the recipient is called Walters, the letter will start with Dear Ms. Walters.

4. **Enter the contents of your letter in the Body field.**

   For guidance on writing your letter, refer to the section called Cover Letters in the advice module included in the Wizard and/or check out the numerous templates and their comments included in the software.

5. **Choose an ending for your letter from the drop-down list at the bottom of the window.**

   Your letter is automatically signed with the first name and last name that you indicated in the Sender window.

6. **Click the Create button to access the software's main window.**

   Your newly created cover letter appears on the right side of the screen.

To add your letter directly to your mailing list, click Add to Mailing List in the Template Management menu.

If you want to edit your cover letter, simply click the template on the main screen to open it in the word processor.

You can also copy your cover letter directly to the Message field in the Mailing List window if it has been written as a Direct E-mail or a Networking Letter. See the section called "Sending your letter and resume by e-mail" to find out more about the Mailing List window.

Modifying an existing template

If the cover letters in the Resumes and Cover Letters For Dummies software don't meet *all* your needs, you can modify one of the many available templates to suit your requirements.

Finding the cover template

You can find a cover letter template to edit in the same folder with the resume templates to edit. Simply browse through the Letters section of the Templates folder within the Templates menu. You can also use the search engine.

Using the search engine

If you're looking for a particular type of letter or resume, you can use the search engine. You can access the search engine by clicking the Find icon in the Template Management menu.

The Find window, as shown in Figure B-11, appears and enables you to enter any key word to find a template matching your needs. Click the Find button and the engine will list all templates matching your search. Click any template to highlight the template in the Templates menu.

Applying template fields

The fields that you define in the active sender profile, as explained in the section titled "Creating your Profile," earlier in this chapter, apply automatically to the letter templates. Therefore, after you select the sender in the Contact Management section and define your profile information, the program automatically displays the corresponding contact details in all the software's letter templates.

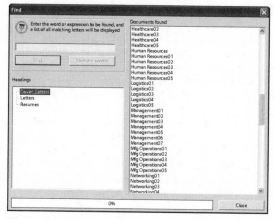

Figure B-11: Using the search engine helps you find the appropriate template easily.

Using the integrated text editor for cover letters

You can customize letter templates by using the integrated text editor. The text editor works much like Microsoft Word. For further details, refer to the section titled "Using the integrated text editor for a resume," earlier in this chapter.

If you want to create a new template, you can start the editor by clicking directly on the New button in the toolbar.

The program then displays a window containing a blank Word-type document in which you can freely compose the letter of your choice. Letters are saved in My Resumes and Cover Letters.

Managing Contacts

One of the neat features of the Resumes and Cover Letters For Dummies software is the ease with which you can add, manage, change, and save your contact information and the contact information of the people to whom you are sending your resumes and cover letters.

The key to accessing these great features lies in the Contact Management menu.

The Contact Management menu provides you with two contact options: one for senders and another for recipients. Both options work in the same way.

If you entered your details the first time you ran the program, your first and last name appear in the Sender section. You can see all of the sender's contact details, which are automatically added to letters, in the Sender Active menu.

To edit a sender's information (such as the phone number), follow these steps:

1. **Click the sender's name in the field below Senders.**

2. **Click the Modify button beneath the name list.**

   The program displays the Senders window.

3. **Make the necessary changes and then click OK.**

Other simple changes that you can make in the Sender section include the following:

- ✔ To delete a sender, click the Remove button.
- ✔ To create a new sender, click the Add button.
- ✔ To create an identical copy of the contact entry, click the Duplicate button.

The option to create an identical copy of a sender is extremely practical because you can create different profiles according to the jobs you're applying for without entering all of your profile details again.

The Recipients option works like the Sender option, with the exception that you can't copy a recipient. Adding a new recipient is simple:

1. **Select the Recipients option in the Contact Management menu.**

2. **Click Add to create a contact entry.**

   The Recipient dialog box appears.

3. **Enter the recipient's information in the applicable boxes.**

4. **After you finish, click OK.**

Printing Your Letter and Resume

After you create your resume, you're ready to print it. Printing your resume couldn't be easier. Just follow these steps:

1. **Select your letter or resume by clicking on it within the Templates tree structure in the Templates menu.**

2. **Click the Print button in the Template Management section.**

   The software displays the Printer Settings window.

3. **Make any necessary adjustments to the printer settings.**

   You can change the paper size in this section, for example.

4. **Click the Print button to print your letter.**

Sending Your Letter and Resume by E-Mail

E-mailing resumes is becoming more and more accepted in the business world, and this mode of delivery can save you money as well. To send your letter or resume by e-mail, just follow these steps:

1. **Click the Add to Mailing List button.**

2. **Click the Mailing List button in the toolbar to display the Mailing List window, as shown in Figure B-12.**

   Your selected letter is automatically added as an attachment. You can check the letters attached in the Attachments section at the bottom of the window.

Figure B-12: Using the Mailing list option enables you to send letters and resumes to multiple recipients easily.

3. Select a recipient from the list in the Recipient field.

The software displays the corresponding e-mail address in the Email Address field.

You can't enter an address from this screen; it has to be entered when filling in the recipient's contact details.

4. Click the Recipient button again to add an additional recipient.

You can send separate e-mails to as many different recipients as you like.

5. **Fill in the subject line, enter the message text, and add your attachment(s).**

6. **Click the Send button to e-mail your letter.**

   A message asks you to confirm; simply click Send.

Using the Organizer

The Organizer feature lets you manage your job search, especially your impending interviews, important dates, and so on. To start the Organizer, simply click the Organizer button on the toolbar.

The Organizer is simple to use:

- ✔ The month is surrounded by two scroll buttons, which enable you to scroll through the months.

- ✔ The left side of the Organizer displays the current month's calendar. If you want to select a specific day, simply click on it.

- ✔ The right side of the Organizer is for entering notes (interviews, deadlines for applications, and so on).

The program automatically saves the notes, which are displayed whenever the day in question is selected. But clicking the Save button after you type out a note is still a good idea.

Similarly, if you want to delete the notes, click the Delete button.

The Minimize button beneath the notes box is extremely useful: It gives you access to your organizer by creating an icon in the Windows system tray (where the clock and sound controls are). That way, you can access your personal organizer, even when you're not using the software.

You can also set an alarm to remind you of an appointment on the appropriate day. Simply select the Alarm option after you write and save your notes. On the day in question, your organizer reminds you that you entered notes for that particular day, even if you're not using the program.

Good Advice for Job-Hunting

Resumes and Cover Letters For Dummies comes with a module that helps you get advice about writing your resume, interviewing, and job-hunting. To run the Advice module, click the Good Advice for Job-Hunting button in the Wizard window.

After the welcoming animation, you see the main screen — a goldmine of tips and advice, as shown in Figure B-13.

In the menu bar, choose the section that you want to check out first (Applications or Job Search) by clicking the corresponding button.

The various topics within your chosen subject (Applications or Job Search) then appear beneath that heading on the left. Click the topic that interests you. Within that topic, you can

✔ **Go straight to a particular paragraph:** The subject's contents are shown at the top of the page; click the required title if you want to go straight to the corresponding paragraph.

✔ **Print the current section:** To print the current section, click the Print button.

✔ **Exit the module:** To exit the module and return to the Wizard, click the cross at the bottom-right corner of the window.

Additional tips on several templates are included in the Templates menu. You find them by selecting Commented Letters or Resumes — comments are under the template on the main screen and help you create resumes and cover letters that grab attention.

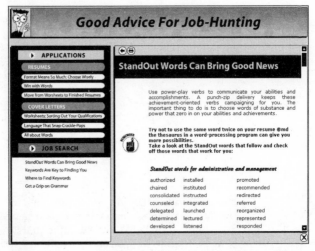

Figure B-13: That module is full of useful advice for both your letters and resumes.

Anuman End-User License Agreement

By using this CD-ROM, you are implicitly agreeing to the following software license. If you disagree with the terms of this license, please return the product in its original packaging to the place where you purchased it.

The following provisions apply to the license and to the warranty. They constitute a legal contract ("License Contract") between you (as an individual or a legal entity) and Anuman Interactive, and its affiliated companies, governing the product and all the accompanying support, software and printed or online documentation. The software is licensed and not sold to you and its use is subject to this License Contract. Anuman Interactive grants you a limited, personal, non-exclusive license to use the software in the manner described in the user documentation.

The license covers all the files on the CD-ROM as well as the present documentation. The entity thus defined will be termed "the Product".

1. Total or partial reproduction of the Product by whatever means is prohibited. Any illegal copy will constitute an infringement of patent, prohibited by international copyright treaties.

2. The Product shall be installed on one computer only, and exclusively for private use.

3. You may not sell (or even give) the user license for the Product to any other party.

4. The rights to the Product are the sole property of Anuman Interactive; they may not be sold or otherwise transferred to any other party.

5. The Product may not be rented, leased or lent out (even free of charge) or publicly displayed or otherwise distributed.

6. The Product may not be transferred from one computer to another or used on any communication network without explicit authorisation from the publisher.

7. The elements that make up the Product, and any documents produced by the acquirer with the aid of these elements, may not be used for commercial purposes.

8. The Product is supplied "as is". Anuman Interactive guarantees that the medium is free of any known defects for a period of ninety (90) days as from the date of purchase. This warranty excludes any dysfunction arising from misuse of the Product. The publisher's financial liability shall under no circumstances exceed the purchase price of the Product.

9. In no event will Anuman Interactive or its employees be liable for any incidental, indirect, special, consequential or punitive damages, or any damages whatsoever (including, without limitation, damages for injury to person or property, for loss of profits, business interruption, loss of business information, loss of privacy, failure to meet any duty and negligence) arising out of or in any way related to the use or inability to use the software, even if the company or an authorized representative of Anuman Interactive has been advised of the possibility of such damages.

10. The data contained in the Product are provided for information only; Anuman Interactive shall not be held liable for any error, omission, or oversight which may be encountered in the Product nor for the consequences, whatever they may be, arising from the use of the data provided.

11. The files on the CD-ROM, and the title of the Product, are the property of Anuman Interactive. This product is protected by copyright laws and by international copyright treaties.

12. Acquirers are entitled to technical support. Anuman Interactive provides through a local provider free technical support by telephone, fax, or e-mail.

13. This License is effective until terminated. You may terminate this License at any time by destroying the Product. This License will terminate automatically without notice from Anuman Interactive if you fail to comply with any provision of this License. All provisions of this License as to warranties, limitation of liability, remedies and damages will survive termination.

14. If any provision or portion of this License is found to be unlawful, void or for any reason unenforceable, it will be severed from and in no way affect the validity or enforceability of the remaining provisions of this License contract.

APPENDIX

Anuman Interactive has signed a License Agreement with Macromedia Inc. concerning the use, reproduction and distribution of the Flash Player software (the Software). This License Agreement is transferred through the present EULA and entails for End User (Licensee) the respect of the following conditions:

- Licensee may not make the Software available as stand-alone products from the Internet.

- Licensee must use the installers provided by Macromedia AS IS and may not modify or alter the way the files are installed without express written permission from Macromedia.

- Other versions of the Software found elsewhere, including on www.Macromedia.com, www.Shockwave.com, or any other download site on the Internet, cannot be distributed under this agreement, including, but not limited to, downloading, distributing, embedding, or any other use of versions of the Software for mobile devices, internet appliances, set top boxes (STB), handhelds, phones, web pads, tablets, game consoles, TVs, DVDs, internet appliances or other internet connect devices, PDA's, medical devices, ATM's, telematics, gaming machines, home automation systems, kiosks or any other consumer electronics device or mobile/cable/satellite/television or closed system operator based service device and for any operating system that is not an Authorized Operating System.

- Licensee may only redistribute the Software through a server, if such redistribution is via an Intranet, and for non-commercial use only. Licensee may not redistribute the Software from a server for use in an operator based commercial service. For example, Licensee may not install and operate the Software even on one of the operating systems specified in Section 1(c) if the Software is used on a server for commercial purposes or for any use.

- Licensee may not combine the Software with Licensee Product in such a way that the Licensee Product's own file format or data type takes over the file format or data type for the Software. The Macromedia Flash Player, Shockwave Player and Authorware Player must always remain the default players for their respective file formats and data types.

- Licensee will not decompile, reverse engineer, disassemble, or otherwise reduce the Software to a human-readable form, modify or create derivative works based upon the Software.

- Licensee will not export the Software into any country prohibited by the United States Export Administration Act and the regulations thereunder. "This Software is 'Restricted Computer Software.' Use, duplication, or disclosure by the U.S. Government is subject to restrictions as set forth in this Agreement and as provided in DFARS 227.7202-1(a) and 227.7202-3(a) (1995), DFARS 252.227-7013 (Oct 1988), FAR 12.212(a)(1995), FAR 52.227-19, or FAR 52.227-14, as applicable." Licensee acknowledges that neither the Software nor the underlying information or technology may be downloaded or otherwise exported or re-exported: (i) into (or to a national or resident of) Cuba, Iraq, Libya, Yugoslavia (Serbia and Montenegro), North Korea, Iran, Syria or any other country to which the U.S. has embargoed goods; or (ii) to anyone on the U.S. Treasury Department's list of Specially Designated Nationals or the U.S. Commerce Department's Table of Denial Orders. Licensee hereby represents and warrants that it is not located in or under the control of, a national or resident of any such country or on any such list.

- Licensee will provide notice of and impose the restrictions in this Section, upon its distributors, resellers, licensees and end users including setting the restrictions forth in an end user license.